IN THE REALM OF RIVERS

Alabama's Mobile-Tensaw Delta

IN THE

of

PUBLISHED BY NEWSOUTH BOOKS

FOR THE ALABAMA COASTAL FOUNDATION

AND WITH THE SPONSORSHIP OF

ExxonMobil	The Crampton Trust
Mobile Bay National Estuary Program	Alabama State Port Authority
Alabama Power Foundation	Riviera Utilities
Taylor Engineering, LLC	Dr. Lynn Yonge
Boan Contracting Company	Leatherbury Real Estate
Mobile Bay Audubon Society	The Nature Conservancy

U.S. Fish and Wildlife Service

REALM
RIVERS

Alabama's Mobile-Tensaw Delta

TEXT BY SUE WALKER ∽ PHOTOGRAPHS BY DENNIS HOLT
FOREWORD BY E. O. WILSON

Published by NewSouth Books
P.O. Box 1588, Montgomery, AL 36102
for the Alabama Coastal Foundation
122 Fairhope Ave., Fairhope, AL 36532

LIBRARY OF CONGRESS CATALOGING-IN-PUBLICATION DATA
Walker, Sue, 1939–
In the realm of rivers : Alabama's Mobile-Tensaw Delta / by Sue
Walker ; photographs by Dennis Holt ; foreword by E.O. Wilson.
p. cm.
ISBN 1-58838-172-2 (alk. paper)
1. Natural history—Alabama—Mobile-Tensaw Delta.
2. Mobile-Tensaw Delta (Ala.) I. Title.
QH105.A2W25 2004
508.761'2—dc22
2004021677

Design by Randall Williams and Breuna Baine
Printed in Korea by Pacifica Communications

*A Tri-colored Heron waits motionlessly
to capture its next meal.*

Contents

Foreword

Edward O. Wilson

WE may count it a small miracle that the Mobile-Tensaw Delta wilderness has survived mostly unscathed into the twenty-first century. Our forebears get no credit for the gift. This marvelous three hundred square-mile sanctuary would have been put to axe and plow generations ago if the powerful flows of the two rivers had not secured it.

A sanctuary, did I say? Yes, of nature and spirit. Imagine, as a thought experiment, that the people of the densely settled Alabama Gulf Coast were to go someplace else and not come back for a hundred years. They would find drastic change everywhere—except in the Delta. A thousand years ago this sprawling habitat was very much the same as it is today. And so it will be, hopefully, a thousand years from now. There have been some changes, of course. The Amerindians of the Mississippian culture who adapted to the swamp interior with mounds and canals are gone. So are Bachman's warbler and most of the cane thickets where the little bird nested. The Alabama sturgeon, which crowded through the main channels until upstream dams blocked their spawning migrations, are now so rare as to be close to extinction. But mostly the fauna and flora of the Delta remain—rich, complex, and immemorial.

What then of spirit? The Mobile-Tensaw Delta is a remnant of Alabama's deep history. The record of any geographical region, such as the Gulf Coast, does not extend back merely for decades or even centuries, but for millennia. To know the land and its people in this totality is to give value to the living world into which people intrude and which they continuously modify to their own ends. The Delta preserves much of what remains of that irreplaceable early record. Its antiquity provides a sense of place, that we have known, that our ancestors knew,

Opposite: *an American alligator, one of the most common residents of the Mobile-Tensaw Delta.*

7

that belongs to us and will be transmitted identically to future generations. It is not just a piece of land with plants and animals. It is a living, dynamical system. All of the Delta is alive, from its teeming waters, where live one of the most diverse array of fishes in North America, to the air above the tree crowns where rare swallow-tailed kites hawk for dragonflies. It remains only partly explored. It is a mystery. Many of the species of insects and other smaller animals living there are still unknown to science. It is far richer in genetic diversity than any of the human-modified habitats surrounding it. We can traverse it, but we still understand it only in bits and pieces.

Those who look more closely and open their senses to the Delta will see a meeting place for science and the humanities, for research and art, a sanctuary to explore and dream, a venue to learn and teach, a playground, and a temple of immeasurable value.

Lexington, Massachusetts
June 2004

Sponsor's Preface

KAY FRIEDLANDER

ONE of the joys of living in southwest Alabama is the proximity of the Mobile-Tensaw Delta. This estuary is a vibrant habitat for fish, turtles, birds, bears, insects, snakes, alligators, pole cats, marsh grasses, flowers, cypress trees, pine trees and much more. Equally interesting are the people and the history of this unique natural resource. When it became clear that there was no single source of information on the natural and cultural history of the Delta, I decided a book was needed.

As fate would have it, I had recently become a member of the Board of Directors of the Alabama Coastal Foundation, and when the board heard me talk about the book idea, the response was a unanimous yes. When Sue Walker agreed to write the text and Dennis Holt signed on as the photographer, it was clear that their love of the Delta would give the book a vivid sense of history, place, and beauty. I am grateful to them for making this idea a reality.

There are many kinds of environmental organizations and each has its special interests and approach to promoting and accomplishing a better world. The approach of the Alabama Coastal Foundation is to educate regarding environmental issues and to partner with municipalities, businesses, organizations, and individuals to bring about resolution. *In the Realm of Rivers: Alabama's Mobile-Tensaw Delta* is a natural fit with ACF's goals to facilitate communication, promote education, and endeavor to increase public understanding and appreciation of the environmental health, cultural heritage, historic sites, aesthetic values, and recreational, and commercial importance of Alabama's coastal resources.

We hope that as this book reveals the many facets of the Mobile-Tensaw Delta, its readers will become active participants in preserving the rich biodiversity of this unique ecosystem. Human impact on the environment can be devastating, but at the same time humans are the solution. By sharing information and working together, we will have cleaner water, will sustain biodiversity, and will maintain the natural beauty of the Delta for generations to come.

Acknowledgments

WE wish to thank those who have worked with us and helped bring this book to fruition: those at Alabama Coastal Foundation, and especially Kay Friedlander, who believed in this project and made it happen, along with Suzanne La Rosa and Randall Williams at NewSouth Books.

Sue wishes to thank George T. Byrne who generously shared his archives and historical collection on Baldwin County and the Delta. His generosity with material, his time, and good spirit, were invaluable. Special thanks to Leslie Smith and Genie Hamner for sound advice, proof reading and friendship, and to Dean David Johnson at the University of South Alabama for his support that enabled time for research and writing. Others who taught her to love words are her grandparents Annie and Web Brannan, who lived on Georgia Avenue and are ever in her heart, along with her grandmother Mary King who used to take her on walks along Magnolia River and taught her to love nature, especially the river. She shall always owe a debt of gratitude too deep for words to her parents, Katie and Louie Brannan. Thanks too to her siblings: Jean, Walt, Lillian, and Larry. Last but first, always, in her heart, are her sons Wesley, James, and Jason, and her husband Ron.

Dennis thanks his dad, Hartley B. Holt, a Methodist minister who first taught him the marvels and mysteries of nature on his field trips as a counselor at Camp Sumatanga in north Alabama. And Dr. Joe Dixon, a physician, friend, and photography mentor who instructed Dennis on photographic discipline. He critiqued Dennis on what he "needed" to be told and not always what he "wanted" to hear. And thanks to Dennis's wife Lynn who allowed him the time to explore and gave him the encouragement to be patient when capturing his images. The job could not have been completed without the assistance of Bob Andrews, Pete and Denise Thomas, Sonny and Autrey Feaster, Mike, Jennifer, and Josh Thompson, and Clyde Eurick, who shared their individual expertise and provided transportation into some of the most remote, scenic, and hard-to-reach areas. Dennis said that his greatest gift received from the Delta may be his opportunity to pass along, show, and teach his first grandchild, Kayla, and her generation, the marvels of nature, as his dad taught him.

IN THE REALM OF RIVERS

Alabama's Mobile-Tensaw Delta

Hiding Tree

In the heart of a tree,

as in the heart of a brother

and a sister, there is space for hiding.

When the wood is dark and the wilderness

taunts with things human beings fail

to understand, limbs reach out to embrace

the sky. Overhead a rainbow is waiting

to happen. The brightest color is teal.

I.

Introduction

THE Mobile-Tensaw Delta—the area in lower Alabama whose border towns include McIntosh, Mount Vernon, and Satsuma on the west and Tensaw and Stockton on the east—is more than a place, an area, a region, a definition, a name. It is more than a landscape, more than three hundred thousand meandering acres. The Delta is more than black prairies, Chunnenuggee hills, flatwoods, southern red hills, buhrstone hills, lime hills, southern pine hills, and soggy swampland that extends from the confluence of the Alabama and Tombigbee rivers as they flow southward to Mobile Bay. The Delta is an estuary, the place where tidal marine waters and the freshwater currents of a river meet the sea. In the case of the Mobile-Tensaw Delta, the Mobile and Tensaw rivers run into Mobile Bay.

The Mobile-Tensaw Delta is one of the largest wetland ecosystems in the United States. It is mysterious, spiritual, beautiful, powerful, and espouses kinship with Mother Earth.

Geomorphically, the Mobile-Tensaw Delta is an alluvial or flood plain and not an actual delta at all. It is Alabama's legacy and trust—a realm of rivers: the Alabama, Tombigbee, Tensaw, Mobile, Blakeley, and Apalachee. It is the locale of lakes: Byrnes, Hastie, Little Chippewa, Silver, Stiggins, and Mifflin; the bound of bayous: Canot and Nenemoosha; and bays: D'Olive, Polecat, and Chocolatta with its variously spelled name. Landings lure people to "put in" at Patrick's, at Hurricane, Clover Leaf, or Chickasaw or to stock up at Busby's Fish Camp, or Shellbank Fish Camp on the "squirt-off" of the Blakeley River not far from Bay Minette. Near Polecat Bay are Autrey's, Sioux, and Stagnes camps, and not far from the Apalachee River, the Red Mastin and Holey Hut fish camps promise fishermen good times ahead. In this wealth of surrounding water, a bounty of speckled trout, redfish, largemouth bass, white shrimp, blue crabs, and mullet make their home.

The Delta is a place of dreams, a place where black bears used to roam, a place where blackbirds, eagles, falcons, and herons take wing. Along the shores and in the swampland grow wild wisteria, water lilies, pickleweed, muscadines, dogwoods, and willows.

The Mobile-Tensaw Delta is also a community, a culture whose history, storied existence, and environment are conveyed through its topology, geology, geomorphology, hydrology. It is a mindscape harbored deep in memory's soil, the trace of all that has shaped the Delta's rich history.

The Delta answers to many names. Bill Finch of the *Mobile Register* once called it "a waterfront trader, a wheeler-dealer, haggling with the river and dickering with the sea." It speaks in a diversity of tongues and flourishes in the quick thrust of language. Pines whisper and sigh, brooks prattle, and bullfrogs grumble and croak. Owls ask "whoooo," and men, women, and children express wonder and awe in words that preserve stories, for it is in such testimonies the Delta thrives.

History and mythology have long referenced the earth as the "Magna Mater," but since the early 1970s the term has become associated with feminist issues. Some ecofeminists specifically reject sexist language that denigrates women by referring to them in such animal terms as chicks, pigs, cows, cats, foxes, snakes—words that deem them bird-brains or classify them as batty. They point out the fact that "virgin timber" is felled, that "fertile soil" is tilled, and that land lies fallow.

Even the term "Mother Earth" is suspect, for as Carolyn Merchant, a professor of environmental history, philosophy, and ethics at the University of California, Berkeley, pointed out in a 1980 text, *The Death of Nature,* "the metaphor of the earth as a nurturing mother was gradually to vanish as a dominant image as the Scientific Revolution proceeded to mechanize and to rationalize the world view." It is time to move beyond classifying and linguistic diffractiveness and to speak instead of synthesization or, to use the naturalist-biologist Edward O. Wilson's term, consilience, the unification of knowledge. It is time to take "care" with words and to take care of the earth, to take care of and nurture the Delta.

Mothering is no longer a woman thing, so instead of conceiving the term as one that designates domination and relegates that which is feminine to a position of inferiority, "Mother," and indeed the "mothering" associated with nurturing, when mentioned, are used to emphasize anew the importance of generation. Mother Earth, of which the Delta is a part, calls for care and preservation, but these attributes are no longer associated solely with a female giving birth.

Edward O. Wilson, in *On Human Nature,* says that

the true Promethean spirit of science in a new age . . . constructs the mythology of scientific materialism, guided by the corrective devices of the scientific method, addressed with precise and deliberatively affective appeal to the deepest needs of human nature, and kept strong by the blind hopes that the journey on which we are now embarked will be farther and better than the one just completed.

When acknowledging archetypal designations of the feminine in reference to rivers and mountains, and when speaking of Gaia herself, it is not, in the name of science, imperative to ignore the pull of myth or to escape verberations and reverberations that attest to an understanding of what the Delta is, what it was, and what it yet may be. Can we fathom, indeed divine, a Mother more than four billion years old? Eric Gould says that myths serve to explain facts about human nature and its worldly or cosmic context. Joseph Campbell postulates that our mythologies are a supply of inexhaustible energy that the cosmos makes manifest, both humanly and culturally.

Deltas have long been sources of fascination. Herodotus, often reputed to be the first historian, born in Greece in 484 B.C., studied the Nile and speculated about its origins. He examined collections of sediments formed by deposits of stream-borne material and described them as being deltoid in shape. Writing about the geomorphology of the Mobile Delta some 2,455 years later, W. Everett Smith notes that the Mobile delta plain, mapped by P. C. Reed in 1971, shows varying sea level elevations and placements of alluvium that go back 10,000 years *(Geomorphology of the Mobile Delta)*.

Deltas are made up of sediments of silt and sand, of clay and cumulations of rock and mineral particles transported by water as it flows and

makes deposits that form an alluvial area at the mouth of a river when it conjoins a larger body of water. Eugene M. Wilson, in his introduction to *Historic Resources Assessment, Mobile and Tensaw River Deltas, Alabama,* notes that the Mobile-Tensaw Delta begins where the Mobile River itself separates into the Mobile River channel on the west and the Tensaw River on the east. It consists of an Upper Delta Flood Plain that lies north of the Tombigbee-Alabama River junction, a Middle Delta Swamp that is a bottomland hardwood forest, and a Lower Delta area of marsh.

Chronology lends perspective to a study of areas such as the Mobile-Tensaw Delta. In 1916, geologist Adolph Knopp made the bold pronouncement that the single greatest contribution to the science of geology lay in a realization of how time was recorded. Mark Twain wrote that "nothing hurries geology," but certainly reckonings of time provide knowledge about the Mobile-Tensaw Delta.

The Mobile-Tensaw Delta was influenced by the glacial melt that occurred in "The Great Ice Age" in the second period of the Cenozoic era in the Pleistocene epoch. During the Pleistocene epoch, some two million years ago, a series of ice ages occurred in which glacial periods lasted thousands of years. During these

periods, glaciers covered much of North America, and it is said that ice formations towered as much as 13,000 feet.

We are presently living in the Cenozoic Era, the time period that goes as far back as 65 million years, a time that extends to the present day. But narrowing the frame further, we designate the last 1.8 million years up to the present time as the Quaternary Period, and place

it within two epochs—the Pleistocene and the Holocene. Referencing Late Pleistocene-Holocene chronology, the Mobile-Tensaw Delta, according to Eugene M. Wilson, fits into the time period 115,000 to 10,000 B.P. In the glacial state of the Pleistocene epoch, the sea level dropped several times. The coastline

of the Gulf of Mexico, formed around 18,000 B.P., was 100 to 110 kilometers farther south. Wilson notes that

the present submerged near-shore region was then forested, and early North Americans occupied this new part of the Coastal Plain. As streams cut deep valleys in response to low sea level, the former Mobile delta and floodplain existed only where the surface remnants had not eroded away. In the period from around 17,000 B.P., sea level rose overall, flooding the coastal zone, filling valleys, and again forming estuaries, bays, barrier islands, and beaches. River gradients became more gentle, and gradually–rapidly in geologic time–flood-

plains and deltas formed again. This time, sea level did not return to its previous position but has remained, so far, about 18 feet lower than the pre-Wisconsin (glacial state of the Pleistocene epoch) high level at 124,000 B.P. ("Mobile Delta Geomorphology," Historic Resources Assessment)

E. M. Wilson says that the Mobile-Tensaw Delta is extending into the head of the bay at a rate of nine hundred feet per century, and during the nineteenth century, it grew some eighteen hundred feet. The oyster beds in the bottom of Mobile Bay appeared around 6,500 B.P. but shifted due to bay salinity toward the lower half of the bay around 4,000 B.P.

It has been said that Time is a teacher whose pupils never hang around very long. Who, indeed, can hold the hands of Time and keep them still, notwithstanding the lament by the English poet Ben Jonson concerning the brevity of human life, when he cried out "for an engine to keep back all clocks."

"Nae man can tether time or tide," writes the poet Robert Burns, though a 1996 Coca-Cola Company annual report published in *National Geographic* said human life appeared on earth a billion hours and a billion minutes ago, while a "billion Coca-Colas ago was just yesterday morning." The Mobile-Tensaw Delta has been around more than 124,000 years, but with the threat of global warning and problems with pollution, the Delta's future lies in preserving this valuable ecosystem.

The poet T. S. Eliot says "time present and time past / are both perhaps present in time future" ("Burnt Norton"). Perhaps, then, we may indulge in a bit of time-traveling and imagine that it is somewhere between A.D. 1100 and 1550. We find ourselves in a Mississippian Culture where Native Americans have con-

Opposite: *aerial overview of the Delta;* **inset:** *nesting egrets.*
Left: *butterflies, a black bear cub, and a bellowing alligator.*

Mississippian artifacts from the Bottle Creek mounds site.

structed amazing complexes of temple mounds. To orient our-selves in present terms, we are situated about a mile east of where the Tensaw and Middle rivers divide, where the Tensaw once divided and formed what is known as Bottle Creek.

Mound Island astounds us with its series of eighteen mounds that rise majestically out of the swamp in stark contrast to the area's surrounding mud and marsh. It is the place where Missis-sippian Indians lived from 1250–1550. The mounds were cer-emonial sites, but they also served as protective high land during spring floods. The mounds still harbor treasured secrets and reveal something of what life was like in the days of an earlier native culture.

Bottle Creek is so heavily forested and so remote that primary access to it is by boat. The mounds are approached, then, by foot, a walk that leads through dense palmettos and a bog that is home to numerous snakes. Suddenly, Mound A, some forty-eight feet high, comes into view. Mounds B, C, D, and E circle around it, as do mounds M and N.

Jean-Baptiste Le Moyne de Bienville once visited this sacred territory of the *petit costeau*, and, according to historian Peter Hamilton, the Indian who delivered de Bienville to the sacred ground had to be bribed with the present of a gun before he would show the explorer the five clay figures of a man, woman, child, bear, and owl once worshiped by tribal Mobilians.

The Bottle Creek area, once owned by the McMillan family, was sold to Scott Paper Company in the early 1900s. It was later donated to the State of Alabama and is now an archaic realm removed from the traffic of the modern world.

The Tomes and the Naniabas, considered Choctaws, were the earliest habitants of the Mobile-Tensaw Delta and preceded Spanish and French infiltration into the area. The "friendly Creeks," descendants of those who once sided with the United States in the Creek War of 1813–14, settled on the Tensaw River, near its junction with the Alabama River.

T. S. ELIOT WROTE that the river "is within us; the sea is all about us." Surely when we travel the Delta's rivers, when we walk along its shores and observe the deer, the heron, bobcats, red-bellied turtles, snakes and ants, we realize at once that we are inside Nature, and Nature is inside us. We use the language of our ancestors and borrow their names: Tombigbee and Alabama, shoring up a past ever present. We say "Tombigbee," perhaps without realizing that it was originally the Choctaw designation *itumbibikpi,* or "Itomba Igaby." The word referred to "an under-taker," the old tribesmen who prepared the "bonehouses," or coffins of the dead. The word gradually became "Tombagaby" and later Tombigbee as we know it today.

Other words such as Alabama, Albama, Alebamon, Alibama, Alibamou, Alibamon, Alabamu, and Allibamou defined the Indian tribe that later became the Muscogee Confederacy. Ac-cording to accounts in the Alabama Department of Archives and History, the word was referenced in accounts of the 1540 expedition of Hernando De Soto by Garcillasso de la Vega who wrote it as Alibamo. The historian Alexander Beauford Meek claimed that Alabama was a Muskogee word that meant "Here We Rest," but the Reverend Allen Wright, a Choctaw scholar, said that the word meant "thicket clearers," for *alba* was the word for a thicket or mass of vegetation, and *amo* meant to clear it or to gather up.

In the gathering of rivers that comprises the Delta, the music of the past resonates in such names as Apalachee, Bayou Tallapoosa, Bayou Canot, and Bayou Matche. Chacaloochee, Chickasabogue, and Little Chippewa roll with pleasure on the tongue and keep alive memories of Alabama's aboriginal settlers.

With the mind's eye, it is possible to set out in a light canoe with Mobile's early explorer, William Bartram, as he named flora and fauna and compiled what would become the book that bears his name, *Bartram's Travels.* It is July 31st, 1775. The air is hot and humid, and the temperature registers 87 degrees as we approach Mobile Bay. It would be hotter still had it not been for the relief afforded by day-long showers of rain. The sound of thunder is in the air as if Thor himself is throwing rocks against Tensaw's bluffs.

"What a sylvan scene is here!" Bartram exclaims. "The pomp-ous Magnolia reigns sovereign of the forests. How sweet the aromatic Illicium groves!" His rapture is contagious as he com-ments on how gaily the radiated wings of the *Magnolia auriculata* flutter. "What a superbly crested silver plume," he says. "What fragrant blossoms, what crimson studded strobile and fruits!"

According to Bartram, the area of lowland swamp is the richest he has ever seen. He says that he "forbears to describe the trees"; they seem incredible. In accord with his Quaker faith, he believes that plants and animals, white man and the Indian, are all part of a "doctrine of light" and blessed with the dignity and

virtue that herald from the Divine. Enthralled with coming upon a veritable Garden of Eden in south Alabama, Bartram revels in naming its vegetation.

Bartram's hands stretch out in reverence. He reaches toward the sky. We hear his voice, soft as the morning air. It is a moment of worship. He gives the plants their name. *"Ash,"* he says. *"Platanus, Populus, Liquidambar."* The words are mellifluous on his tongue. Suddenly, he hesitates, looking up at trees that tower above him. They are enormous, the tallest and straightest his eyes have ever seen. Even the reeds and cane stand thirty or forty feet tall. "They are as thick as a man's arm," he exclaims. "I believe they're as much as three or four inches in diameter."

Nature is the ultimate artist, painting the Delta in a majestic blend of color. A single sunset can contain everything cardinal: rouge and carmine, scarlet and claret and port, vermillion, russet, cherry, murrey and maroon, coral, salmon, cochineal, auburn. In the Delta, the truest Titian sky is flushed, hot, feverish, burning, glowing, ruddy-red, indeed incarnadine.

Such singular beauty that startled Bartram into seeming disbelief is not all of the naturalist's story as he travels the Alabama Delta. In the vicinity of Tensaw Bluff he discovers the evening primrose and says that it is "the most pompous and brilliant herbaceous plant known to exist."

Bartram stands before the Bald Cypress in rapt attention. He takes in its size, measures its trunk and looks up, up, up, maybe eighty or ninety feet where an eagle is nesting. To Bartram, the tree is emblematic of America. Later, he writes:

> The *Cupressus disticha* stands in the first order of North American trees. Its majestic stature is surprising; and on

Opposite: *Bottle Creek Indian Mound.* **This page:** *a moonlit scene on the Bartram Canoe Trail.* **Overleaf:** *paddlers on the Trail.*

approaching it, we are struck with a kind of awe, at beholding the stateliness of the trunk, lifting its cumbrous top towards the skies, and casting a wide shade upon the ground, as a dark intervening cloud, which, for a time, excludes the rays of the sun . . . forming a grand straight column eighty or ninety feet high, when it divides every way around into an extensive flat horizontal top like an umbrella, where eagles have their secure nests, and cranes and storks their temporary resting places . . .

Two hundred years later, the Bartram Trail is one of the natural wonders of Alabama. If we follow the Bartram Trail, take a field trip into the wilderness, we might find the cow parsnip, *Quercus hemisphaerica*; the dwarf saw palmetto that Bartram named *Corypha repens*, today designated *Serenoa repens*, and the pyramid magnolia, *Magnolia pyramidate*.

The sixteen-mile water route stretches along the Tensaw River from Hubbard's Landing to Live Oak Landing in the Stockton area.

The Delta does not belong to humankind although human beings have intruded upon it. In this rich haven, mud squishes under the pad of paw; hunters walk gingerly, and try not to disturb dry leaves. Crickets hum, mosquitoes whine, squirrels chitter, and crows call out in response to the rain's patter, the calming babble of brooks and the melody of singing birds. Thomas Merton, in "Rain and the Rhinoceros," a treatise commenting upon the innumerable attributes of a many-voiced landscape, said,

Think of all that speech pouring down, selling nothing, judging nobody, drenching the thick mulch of dead leaves, soaking the trees, filling the gullies and crannies of the wood with water, washing out the places where men have stripped the hillside. . . . It will talk as long as it wants, the rain. As long as it talks I am going to listen.

The Delta needs human ears to hear its speech, and it needs human hands to write the lisp of lips, to speak of the fury of hurricane winds, to describe the roughness of bark, trace the veins of leaves, and remark on the sharp pine needles. It needs the human tongue to capture the magic and mystery of traces and trails, twigs and tattoos, the calligraphic scrawl of rivers and creeks and streams. Nature's scribbles leave their mark and are part of a memory book recorded in the brain and writ in parchment derived from trees.

Perhaps if we squint in the sunlight of the mind's bright eye, we can still see the "line of demarcation" that fixed the United States / Spanish West Florida boundary at the thirty-first parallel.

An appointee of President George Washington, Major Andrew Ellicott, a Philadelphia engineer and Surveyor General of the United States, is commissioned to conduct a survey that would take an arduous four years to complete. After leaving Philadelphia on September 16, 1786, en route to Natchez, Ellicott made his way to Little and Big Bayou Sara, and on March 17, 1789, he arrived in Mobile.

The Delta contains one survey monument, the Ellicott Stone. This National Landmark can be found on the west side of the Mobile-Tensaw river. It is three feet high, two feet wide, half a foot thick and marks the place designated by Major Ellicott in 1799 as the thirty-first parallel.

Left: *State of Alabama historical marker.*
Right: *Ellicott's Stone is a National Landmark.*

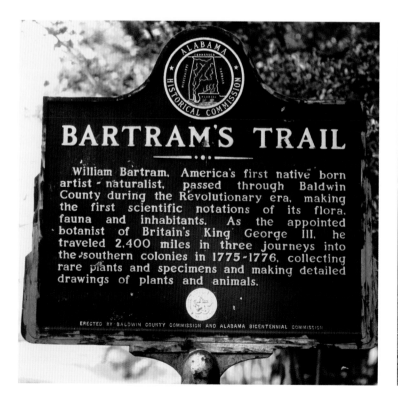

THE MOBILE-TENSAW DELTA cradles history in its arms and does not make distinctions as to the peculiar "nature" of those who travel its woods and wilds. One infamous and errant traveler who possessed a talent for capturing the sweet sentiments of women is the murderer of Alexander Hamilton, the infamous Aaron Burr, Vice President of the United States. In a disastrous duel that ended the life of the Federalist who opposed his bid for President of the United States in 1800, Burr settled his disagreement by ending Alexander Hamilton's life and, at the same time, his own political career.

Later, Burr moved to the West with a band of armed men in an effort to get Great Britain and Spain interested in claiming enough land to create another country. After a brief return to Washington, he found himself accused of treason. In 1805, a proclamation placed a $2,000 bounty on his head. He escaped from Washington and fled south, eventually stealing into Alabama where he was captured in the Mobile-Tensaw Delta.

Imagine a bitter cold Delta morning. It is February 19, 1807. Captain Edward P. Gaines is alerted of Aaron Burr's whereabouts, and when he goes out to search the area, he finds a stranger hiding in a hollow. He is dressed in earthy pantaloons dyed with copperas (the green iron sulfate used as a fixative in the process of dyeing), wears a roundabout jacket of drab cloth and a wide-brimmed, somewhat shabby beaver hat, and he is none other than Aaron Burr himself.

It is said that Burr's feverishly bright eyes gave him away. Albert J. Pickett, in his 1851 *History of Alabama*, reports that "they

Aaron Burr

shone like stars." Pickett dramatically relates the woodland meeting of Captain Edward P. Gaines and the stranger who was none other than Aaron Burr:

GAINES: I presume, sir, I have the honor of addressing Colonel Burr.

STRANGER: I am a traveler in the country, and do not recognize your right to ask such a question.

GAINES: I arrest you at the instance of the Federal government.

STRANGER: By what authority do you arrest a traveler upon the highway, on his own private business?

GAINES: I am an officer of the army. I hold in my hands the proclamations of the President and the Governor, directing your arrest.

STRANGER: You are a young man, and may not be aware of the responsibilities which result from arresting travelers.

GAINES: I am aware of the responsibilities, but I know my duty.

Knowing that it would be impossible to escape, Burr mounts his horse and rides alongside his captors to Fort Stoddard, built in 1799 to protect Americans living on the Tombigbee River. He remains at the Fort until he is placed in a boat and rowed up the Alabama River, into Lake Tensaw, to arrive finally at Boatyard near Fort Mims. Pickett's words set the scene and read like a modern novel. He writes:

They left the Boat Yard, a quarter of a

mile from which the terrible massacre of Fort Mims afterwards occurred, and, pursuing the Indian path, encamped the first night in the lower part of the present county of Monroe. The only tent taken along was pitched for Burr, and under it he lay the first night by large fires, which threw a glare over the dismal woods. All night his ears were saluted with the fierce and disagreeable howling of wolves. In the wilds of Alabama, in a small tent, reposed this remarkable man, surrounded by a guard, and without a solitary friend or congenial spirit. He was a prisoner of the United States, for whose liberties he had fought; and an exile from New York, whose statutes and institutions bore the impress of his mind.

Pickett says that Burr was no common man, for he "rose in the morning with a cheerful face, and fell into traveling order, along with the taciturn and watchful persons who had charge of him." Ladies who saw the ex-Vice President as a captured prisoner wept in spite of the fateful chain of events that led to his

capture. Pickett sums up his report, "We do not wish to be considered as the defender of Aaron Burr, we do not admire his character . . . but, as a historian, we are expected to write the truth, even if that truth is unpalatable to the prejudices of the age."

LET US CONTINUE our mind's-eye tour of the Delta, cross the Ellicott Line just north of Stockton, and travel the Historic Mims Highway to Tensaw. Here we will turn east on Route 80, and forget the feeling of being lost. We'll continue past trailer parks laying claim to the wilderness, and then, so unassuming that it might be missed, come of a sudden upon a stately marker that reads: FORT MIMS 500 YARDS AWAY.

The story of Fort Mims in the Mobile-Tensaw Delta is part of the consciousness of history. It exists today as a multi-storied landscape whose soil bears witness to one of the country's most horrendous massacres.

Imagine the terrain. The year is 1813. The stockade around Samuel Mims's house, begun with the arrival of the first elements of the Mississippi Territorial Volunteers, which was intended to

Above: *replica of the stockade wall at present-day Fort Mims.*
Opposite: *the historical stone marker at the site.*

be a defense against the Creeks, would prove woefully inadequate against an assault by warring Indians. Potato fields and flat land lay to the south. To the east there were ravines and cane marsh, and to the west, forest land and beyond it, there was Boatyard Lake and the Alabama River

The day is August 30, 1813. It is morning. Lynn Hastie, in her definitive *William Weatherford: His Country and His People*, comments on the scene. On the morning of the battle, the sun hides sporadically behind gray protesting clouds. Nothing seems amiss, but things are not as they seem to the inhabitants of the

Fort Mims stockade. Shirts drying on ropes hold out their arms to the breeze. No one knows that nearby, hiding in the marsh, the forest, the ravines, Indians can smell bacon cooked for breakfast by women in the fort. Major Daniel Beasley, recovering from having imbibed too much the night before, sits at his writing desk around 10:00 a.m. and pens a letter to Brigadier-General Ferdinand Leigh Claiborne at Fort Stoddard. He has improved the fort, he says, and he knows that he will be able to maintain it against any number of Indians. He says that the reports of lurking Indians are false, reaches for a jug of whiskey, and fills his glass.

Nearby, one thousand warriors with faces and bodies ablaze in war paint hear the designated call of a hawk. It is the sign promised by the warrior Peter McQueen that it is time to attack. The poorly prepared fort is doomed.

Historians debate the feelings of William Weatherford, Chief Red Eagle, in regard to the attack. Lynn Hastie says the massacre wore heavily on his mind, especially when it came to hacking, butchering, and scalping women and children. In his 1851 *History of Alabama,* Albert James Pickett asserted that some 550 people had been killed in the worst massacre in American history up to that point. Other period accounts put the death toll at 250, not counting "Redsticks." Historian Peter Hamilton, writing in *Colonial Mobile,* states that "the blood of grey-headed Sam Mims [cries] from the ground," but his spirit, Hamilton says, leads on and opened "the interior of Alabama civilization."

The site remained in private hands until 1954, when it was acquired by the state. In 1917, the U.S. Daughters of 1812 erected a monument at Fort Mims to the victims slaughtered in the battle, and in 1959, the Fort Mims Chapter of the Daughters of the American Revolution erected the monument currently at the site. Perhaps, as Native American legend would have it, the souls of those who died in the massacre hover over the abiding dust still present in the Mobile-Tensaw Delta.

Hamilton's *Colonial Mobile* notes that the southern third of the Delta "is subject to overflow" but that looming bluffs where the Alabama and Tombigbee rivers converge are promising for habitat. The shadows cast by cottonwood trees are reflected in the Mobile River. There are willows too, he says, and forests of pine and oak and beds of oysters as well as abundant crabs, white trout, mackerel, sheephead, sharks and porpoises, alligators, trout, bream, catfish, perch, deer, bear, wolves, and small game.

This idyllic place, named Blakeley after the man who founded it in 1814, became a ghost town during the 1830s. Kay Nuzum, in her 1971 *A History of Baldwin County,* claims that Blakeley "is perhaps the 'deadest dead' town not only in Baldwin County but also in all of Alabama." The town is located in the lower Mobile-Tensaw Delta, about five miles north of Spanish Fort, and some twelve miles from Mobile.

The June 25, 1974, National Register of Historic Places reports that Blakeley was founded January 6, 1814, when "the Mississippi Territorial Legislature authorized Josiah Blakeley and a group of New England businessmen to plat a town to be located at the head of the Appalachee [sic] River where it leaves the Tensaw." The town was incorporated in 1815. The harbor, thought to be superior to that of Mobile, brought people to Blakeley.

Nuzum says that Josiah Blakeley was thought to have been a bachelor "who had no wife to double his pleasures or divide his cares." Seeking adventure, he reportedly left Connecticut in the late 1790s to travel from Cuba and from there to the woodland paradise on Mobile Bay that he would designate his home.

Among moss-covered oaks, Blakeley designed lots that measured 99 feet by 199 feet. They bordered 40-foot-wide Water Street and 60-foot-wide Pearl Street, not far from the harbor that led out into the Bay. The town of Blakeley would soon rival Mobile as a place to live and prosper. The *Blakeley Sun,* one of Alabama's earliest newspapers, published by Gabriel F. Mott in 1818, boasted that the town had somewhere between 4,000 and 8,000 habitants and rapturously exclaimed:

> What a wonderful country is ours! How like enchantment towns and villages rise up! Blakeley, eighteen months ago, was a wilderness of impenetrable woods . . . . Nothing is now seen or heard but the din of business and the stroke of the ax resounding in the distant woods—buildings raising their heads in almost every quarter of town, and the constant arrival and departure of vessels present a scene both interesting and beautiful to the contemplative mind and the man of business.
>
> We find no hesitation in saying that Blakeley before many years will be the chief seaport in the Alabama Territory. (qtd. in Nuzum 74 and in L/J. Newcomb Comings and Martha M. Albers *A Brief History of Baldwin County*)

Blakeley could not live up to such grand predictions, and though it prospered for awhile, several factors contributed to the town's demise. A businessman from New England, Thomas Lawrence Hallett, thought that he would ship ready-made houses into the area, but found that land prices soared after Josiah Blakeley got wind of the deal. Hallett, then, redirected his schooner filled with goods to Mobile and established business there. This event brought on an economic depression, and according to Nuzum, "marked the beginning of Blakeley's ending."

The dredging of Pinto Pass was another contributing factor that brought about Blakeley's demise. The Pass enabled ships seeking to transport goods to sail into Mobile more easily than into Blakeley.

I T WAS NOT KNOWN in the 1800s that a mere insect could devastate a town, but two yellow fever epidemics, one in 1826 and another in 1830, caused people to believe that the air was bad and that it, in no small way, was responsible for sickness and disease. Many people died and those who could moved to Mobile, Pensacola, or to higher and more northerly climes. Because of these difficulties, Blakeley, according to the 1974 report of the National Register of Historic Places, was totally abandoned.

Although yellow fever cannot be totally responsible for turning Blakeley into a ghost town, it no doubt deserves a major portion of blame. Dracula has nothing on the female *Aedes Aegypti,* for in this mosquito species, it is the bloodsucking female mosquito, not the male, that transmits the disease. In the 1820s and '30s, however, little was known about the "Saffron Knight," as yellow fever was called in the Mobile-Tensaw Delta area, but some like Dr. Josiah Nott of Mobile suspected that the pesky insect might have something to do with it.

Even though some ecologists believe that everything, animal and insect alike, deserves the right to life, it is hard to promote the cause of *Aedes Aegypti* that belongs to the order Diptera. The female demands a blood feast from which she obtains the protein necessary for the production of eggs. The male simply sips nectar from flowers, has a feathery antennae, and lacks the accoutrement necessary for penetrating skin. She, on the other hand, has a long piercing proboscis, and though she prefers birds, cows, horses, and select savory small animals, she will bite available humans. The crepuscular feeder who dines in the early morning and feasts at night can travel some distance from her original breeding source for a hearty meal.

Mosquitoes have been acknowledged for a long time. Aristotle, referring to them in his *Historia Animalium* of 300 B.C., studied what he called the *empis* life cycle. [See Tom Floore, "Mosquito Information," http//www.mosquito.org/ MosqInfo/ mosquito. html.] The word mosquito is of North American origin. The Spanish called the insects, "flies" or *musketas*. Native Hispanic Americans referred to them as *zancudos*.

IN THE 1860S, during the Civil War, Blakeley again came into prominence and served as a fort that housed 3,500 Confederate soldiers. The town, it is to be noted, is spelled *Blakeley,* the same as its founder's name. The Fort, however, is *Blakely,* without the last "e." (This spelling occurs only during the Civil War.) The actual town was captured a few hours after the surrender of General Robert E. Lee at Appomattox Courthouse in Virginia on April 9, 1865. The Siege of Blakeley had begun on April 2. Although the signing of the Peace Treaty by General Robert E. Lee and General Ulysses S. Grant at the home of Wilmer McLean had already brought an official end to the War, the final battle at Blakeley occurred six hours afterwards.

The sad and unnecessary eight-day siege pitted Union General E. R. S. Canby against Confederate Major General Dabney Maury. The final brief Battle of Blakely followed the Battle of Mobile Bay and the fall of Fort Gaines, Fort Morgan, and Spanish Fort. Hundreds of Confederates ran for shelter in the

Venerable cypress knees.

woods; others drowned in Blakeley River in their attempt to escape. More than three thousand soldiers and three general officers were captured.

The land bears witness and harbors history in hills and ravines, in mounds and trenches, in reflections in water. What once *was* and what *is* and *will be* become common ground. The words of Union Army Commander General C. C. Andrews were prophetic when he said on April 9, 1865, that "over the fields of Blakeley, the bushes are beginning to grow up, and in a few years another forest will no doubt cover the ground. But many of the trenches will remain. The storms of the centuries will not wear them away" (*A History of the Campaign of Mobile*).

Blakeley's ecological terrain provides another perspective from which to view what happened in April 1865. Human nature and Nature construct meaning in cultural scapes of accountability.

The topology of the Delta played a role in the tactical planning of war, for it aided troop maneuverability. George S. Waterman of the Confederate Navy took pains to describe the terrain, commenting that Blakeley was situated "ten miles northeast of Mobile, on the left bank of the Tensas river, which [. . .] deflects to the westward, seeing the bay. It is distant four and one-half miles north of Spanish Fort" (*The Siege of Blakeley*). He spoke

of the mile-and-a-half area of dry ground fronting the river and of the "low and swampy [area] densely covered with hardwood timber and a rank growth of weeds and vines." Such information enabled him to make his battle plans.

Strategically, the bluffs along the river proved formidable in this eight-day siege. General Canby had to conduct a land battle and needed to control the bluffs whose sandy and slimy clay walls extended as high as seventy feet. The cliffs were particularly hazardous. A foot could slip, the wall could crumble, and a soldier could find himself plummeting sixty or more feet into the water below. Snakes and alligators swam the rivers, creeks, and streams. Nature had to be dealt with, and winning a battle meant cutting down trees, digging trenches, ditches, and black mole furrows. At the beginning of the siege, the troops of Brigadier General John P. Hawkins "had to cross an abrupt, deep, broken ravine, made doubly difficult, by a dense tangle of undergrowth" (*Baldwin County Historical Society Quarterly,* II:2, January 1975). The first resistance of Confederate forces took place where a stream ran northwest through a deep narrow ravine that led into wooded swampland. The Confederates occupied the bluff that

Civil War reenactment of the Battle of Blakeley.

bordered on the swamp, and the terrain made it difficult for Colonel J. B. Jones to dislodge them and for reinforcements to be brought in.

On day two of the siege, Major General C. C. Andrews writes that although the ground between the combatants appeared to be level, it was not. He says that it was "cut up by ravines, the sides of which were scalloped with numerous and deep depressions" (*Baldwin County Historical Society Quarterly,* II:2, January 1975). Brooks and streams that ran clear at the bottoms of the ravines were "half concealed by luxuriant bushes and vines." The impact of the environment did not go without notice, for Andrews reported that the good water supply and the density of the wood made his position favorable.

In south Alabama, the weather in April sometimes is still cold and seems to be fighting a battle with the advent of spring. On the eighth day of April 1865, the seventh day of the siege, rain fell. The air was chilly, and Andrews noted that "duty in the muddy trenches was uncomfortable" (*Baldwin County Historical Society Quarterly,* II:2, January 1975). While the wilderness, the marsh and swamp can be deemed beautiful, wild, and free, it can also be a place of danger. Military command and human laws cannot overrule or control the forces of nature, and such natural forces as hurricanes, wind and rain, heat and cold, dictate the actions of men and animals. Man's roots inextricably entwine with those of nature.

The words of Alabama native Margaret Walker, one of the South's prominent African-American authors, are applicable to Blakeley, to both town and battleground, for they are what Walker calls a "Sorrow home." The thriving town fell in ruin, and scars of battle give evidence of a conflict that never should have been fought. Today, this area nestled in the southern part of the Mobile-Tensaw Delta is a living presence, a changed and ever-changing place. Margaret Walker says,

our roots are deep in Southern life; deeper than John Brown or Nat Turner or Robert Lee. I was sired and weaned in a tropic world. The palm tree and banana leaf, mango and coconut, breadfruit and rubber tree know me. Warm skies and gulf blue streams are in my blood. I belong with the smell of fresh pine, with the trail of coon, and the spring growth of wild onion (*Literature and the Environment*).

SINCE 1981, historic Blakeley has been a State Park, and the sites of the battle that took place in the heart of the Delta are part of the Civil War Discovery Trail that opened in 1995. Reenactments of the battle remind us, as William Faulkner said, that the past is never dead. We can only hope to master its lessons.

In Faulkner's *The Sound and the Fury,* Harvard students asked Quentin Compson to tell them about the South: What is it like there? What do they do there? Why do they live there? Students studying with E. O. Wilson at Harvard might well have asked the former Alabamian and author of two Pulitzer-Prize-winning books similar questions about the Mobile-Tensaw Delta. What is it like there? What snakes thrive and slither in the marsh? What fish swim in Nenemoosha Bayou? What birds nest in bald cypress trees? Have you ever eaten rattlesnake meat?

Some questions are answered in Wilson's memoir, *Naturalist,* when he says that a child has a natural sense of wonder and awe. As he speaks of his childhood, he reminisces about his grandmother May as she stands on her porch on Charleston Street in Mobile. He tells of charging out on his Schwinn bicycle to explore the Mobile-Tensaw Delta on old U.S. 90 as far as Spanish Fort. He says he biked into the uninhabited woodland to collect butterflies and survey alligator gars, soft-shelled turtles, fire ants, and snakes. Had those Harvard boys been part of his Boy Scout troop in the summer of 1943, they would have called out "Snake, snake" when they spotted a moccasin slithering through

pickleweed. They would have stood back in awe as Wilson grabbed a stick to pin the snake's body close to its head before rolling it forward and pressing it to the ground. Perhaps they would even let out a triumphant yell as he picked the snake up behind the head and boldly held it up as trophy for them to view. They would have listened as he spoke of the diversity of species living so close at hand and uttered such fancy names as *sistrurus miliarius* when referring to the pygmy snake. Although it is generally only fifty centimeters in length, Wilson explains, it is still poisonous. Once he was he struck by one as he reached his hand somewhat carelessly into the rattlesnake's cage. "Like a quarrel spring from a crossbow," he says, "it uncoiled and struck the tip of my index finger." A nearby doctor in Mobile made an X-shaped cut on his finger, applied a rubber cup, and extracted the venom. With an ear bent in Wilson's direction, those listening would have heard just what this fourteen-year-old future

Blakeley State Park today, near where the last battle of the Civil War was fought.

world-acclaimed entomologist said about Camp Pushmataha and pygmy rattlesnakes, and they would have learned about the Mobile-Tensaw Delta that is a source of wonder, spirituality and joy.

E. O. Wilson says that we are approaching a new age of synthesis, and he believes the testing of consilience is the "greatest of all intellectual challenges" (*Consilience*). This dream of unified learning joins the sciences and the humanities, art and story, geography, geology, biology, archeology, ecology, sociology, botany, linguistics, environmental policy, and ethics. These topics of study are ever present and ready-at-hand, and Wilson's consilience thus provides a lens through which the Mobile-Tensaw Delta may be viewed. ✺

Incident of War: A Letter to President Harding from Charles Hall of Blakeley, Alabama

(A found poem: for George Thomas Byrne, Jr, grandson
of Charles Hall, and Wesley Byrne, his great grandson)

Dear President Harding:

General Edward R. S. Canby was in command
of the Federal Army when the Confederate's last stand
in the War Between the States resulted in surrender.
My father's plantation was destroyed, the discomfiture
is beyond, almost, my ability to write.
On the 11th of April, about 12:00 midnight,
some thirty Federal soldiers came to Papa's house
about nine miles above Fort Blakely and did roust
him, sleeping, from his very bed,
beat him roundly on the head
and with rifles kick him sore about.
Mother and children started to cry and shout
as a scowling soldier deigned to take from her a candle.
It was too much for her frail frame to handle
and she fell upon the floor with the babies, in a heap
and asked only that the soldier let her keep
her young ones safe from harm, whereupon they set fire
to the dwelling house, making a funeral pyre
of it and cottages nearby. Our treasures, too, are gone,
even the wearing apparel we had on.

The next day, broken hearted, his world burned out,
Papa went straightway to the fort, to scout
thereabout, find General Canby
and address him face to face, with dignity,
and relay the misfortune that had come to pass.
The General listened, somewhat aghast,
and said that he would give our family
food to eat and a wagon load of fruit and meat.

I was not, as now, in my sixty-ninth year;
I was only ten and seven months, then, I fear.
It is time to move beyond fear and hate,
and with resolve, I demonstrate
that what was done we all forgave
and place a wreath on Canby's grave.

— Charles Hall

* This poem was based on an actual letter that the Late Judge Charles Hall of Bay Minette wrote to the President in which he said: "General Canby was in command of the Federal Army at Fort Blakely, Alabama. The Confederate soldiers surrendered to him April 9, 1865, and my father and I later went to General Canby for food. He gave us a wagon load. My father's plantation was destroyed by the soldiers and we had no food for the family—my mother and brothers and sisters. For many years I have wanted to place a wreath on General Canby's grave. I am now in my sixty-ninth year and I want to place a wreath on his grave before I pass away." Printed in an Indianapolis paper in 1923 and reprinted in *A Brief History of Baldwin County*, by N. J. Newcomb Comings and Martha M. Albers, (Fairhope, Alabama, March 1928).

Opposite: *Civil War reenactors of the Battle of Blakeley.*

*Brilliant blooms adorn
cardinal flower.*

II.

Inside the Delta

THE Mobile-Tensaw Delta is a place of correspondences, a diverse community shared by plants and animals, birds, fish, creatures the poet Vivian Smallwood referred to as scaly, feathery, or furred. It is a place of assimilation that registers the body as a work of art, a living text, a wild-word wilderness comprised of image, essay, story and poem, a shared environment. Indeed, Thomas Huxley called living nature not a mechanism, but a poem. Naturalist Barry Lopez, in "A Literature of Place," says that "we keep each other alive with our stories. We need to share them, as much as we need to share food. We also require for our health the presence of good companions. One of the most extraordinary things about the land is that it knows this—and it compels language from some of us so that as a community we may converse about this or that place, and speak of the need."

The Mobile-Tensaw Delta is Nature, but it is also Art writ large, a tableau, words like a sunset spread against the sky, lines that bear the print of paw, the flight of an eagle, the fin of a fish in its element. And stating it another way, Nature is Art in a constant act of renewal, yet we must love it enough to preserve it. Art is likewise preservation.

DELTA WILDERNESS, DELTA WILD

Leave Mobile, Alabama, and cross the Causeway heading east toward Blakeley State Park. Get off Interstate 65 and head for Stockton. Choose a landing as a starting point for exploring the Mobile-Tensaw Delta, either Live Oak Landing, Patrick's Landing, Cliff's Landing, Byrne's Landing, Hubbard Landing, or Clover. Grab some bait—and insect repellent should it be summer and mosquitoes are at "high-whine." Pull in at a fish camp: Busby Fish Camp, Holey Hut Fish Camp, Autrey's Camp, Sioux Fish Camp, or put in at Polecat Bay or Chuckfee

Bay, Crab Creek, or Oak Bayou—the wilderness is at hand.

Henry David Thoreau wrote that "in wildness is the preservation of the world," but what does wildness mean? Is *wildness* the same as "wilderness," one word substituting for the other? What Thoreau spoke of as "Tawny Grammar" in his essay, "Walking," is that "vast, savage, howling mother of ours, Nature, lying all around, with such beauty, and such affection for her children, as the leopard; and yet we are so early weaned from her breast to society." Thoreau's grammar brings into discourse a kind of speaking that is not fundamentally *wild*. Rather it gathers knowledge that is representative of science, culture, and civilization. What if we bandy words about, often without consideration of meaning, saying: "Isn't that wild?" Can we actually say that science is *wild*? Is civilization ever *wild*? Is culture *wild*? Poets such as Gary Snyder who write specifically about ecology say that wilderness is "the essential nature of nature." Snyder says, "the way to see *with* language, to be free with it and to find it a vehicle of self-transcending insight, is to know both mind and language extremely well and to play with their many possibilities without any special attachment."

Language is a pirogue, a canoe, a boat with an outboard motor. It takes us into the wilderness where we see the moss, our earth mother's hair, hanging from trees, see the long gray strands of it reflected in water. We look into the eyes of a red-bellied turtle that immediately tucks its head deep into its shell before easing it forward again to peer back at us, its gaze returning our own, wordlessly saying that it is "at home." We are uninvited guests in this wilderness of ours. We are *sans terre*, this word, borrowed from Thoreau's essay "Walking." This word heralds the middle ages when saunterers en route to the holy land were *à la sainte-terre*. According to Thoreau, children shortened the

Opposite: a view off Stiggins Lake.

phrase to "There goes a *saint terrer*" a wanderer without a home. To become "at home" in the woods is a seeking of holy land, and to be a *saint terrer* is a noble, good thing. It is to marvel at alligators nesting, while keeping a safe and respectful distance as we compare their "hide" to our own thin vulnerable skin. Overhead, a crow "caws," and we realize that our tawdry grammar can only take us so far in understanding "wildness."

The Wilderness Act, PL 88-577, Sec 2(c) offers further insight into *wilderness*. It says that:

> a wilderness, in contrast with those areas where man and his own works dominate the landscape, is hereby recognized as an area where the earth and its community of life are untrammeled by man, where man is himself a visitor who does not remain. An area of wilderness is further defined in this Act as an area of Federal land retaining its primeval character and influence, without permanent improvements or human habitation, which is protected and managed so as to preserve its natural conditions and which (1) generally appears to have been affected primarily by the forces of nature, with the imprint of man's work substantially unnoticeable; (2) has outstanding opportunities for solitude or a primitive and unconfined type of recreation; (3) has at least five thousand acres of land or is of sufficient size as to make practicable its preservation and use in an unimpaired condition; and (4) may also contain ecological, geological, or other features of scientific, educational, or historical value.

The Wilderness Act attempts to incorporate and preserve that which is addressed in literature, in essays, poetry, novels pertaining to the "Wild." It adopts the disordered, the unruly and disorganized which in the Early Teutonic and Norse languages was *wil, that which was uncontrollable and even willful.* It claims heir to the word *wilder* that means to be lost and the Old Englsih

wil-deor-ness that signifies a place where wild beasts roam.

Is birdsong wild? Dutch biologists at Leden University who have studied birdsong report that city birds who must make their mating calls heard over the din and thrum of traffic raise the pitch of their song whereas birds in the wilderness sing in a lower register. The study is reported to be the first to show that the noise of "city life" alters the way birds communicate. Additionally, it suggests that if birds are unable to modify their voices, they suffer from it.

Is poetry *wild?* Is art? How do we classify the *wild clematis?* What about the buckeye, the needle palm and the iguana hackberry that enjoy the limey decomposition of an area of shellmounds? Is the river that meanders and never sleeps an example of wildness? Perhaps it is not too wild to claim that human beings need a new way of seeing that which is so old they fail to take it in and attend to it anymore. The poet William Blake speaks of seeing the world in a grain of sand and heaven in a wildflower. Nature is within, and experiencing it thus brings a sense of renewal.

Aristotle believed that poetry was the most philosophic of all writing. Its object, he thought, was truth. The poet Wordsworth claimed that poetry was an acknowledgment of the beauty of the universe, and Samuel Taylor Coleridge, in *Biographia Literaria,* wrote that the poet "brings the whole soul of man into activity."

THE STATUS OF A WILDERNESS like that of the Mobile-Tensaw Delta has been and is changing. When addressing what is meant by "wild," some, like Tom Gause and Davida Hastie say it is less wild than it used to be. What is seen today from a double-ender is not what Bartram saw or Ellicott or Red Eagle or even Aaron Burr when their footprints were upon the land. Ogalala Sioux Chief Luther Standing Bear noted that Native Americans do not recognize the same wilderness as that of white men who settled the "Wild, Wild West." He said that Native Americans did not "think of the great open plains, the beautiful rolling hills, and winding streams with

The summer sun sets north of Mobile off Chacaloochee Bay.

tangled growth as 'wild.'" It is the white man who thinks of nature as a "wilderness," who thinks of the land in terms of "wild" animals.

"Wild" and "Wilderness" are terms that we must re-conceive both literally and linguistically. Environmentalist John Muir says in *Wild Wool* that "Nature is a crab and culture is an orchard apple." He says that going back to the wild renders us astringent or "crabbed." In our "wild" selves, we are unfertilized, unpruned, tough and resilient, but most importantly, we are, each spring, "shockingly beautiful in bloom." He says that most people these days are orchard apples, "cultivated stock," but we can, he says, "stray back into the woods."

The final word, here, belongs to poet Gary Snyder, who, in *The Practice of the Wild*, concludes:

> The lessons we learn from the wild become the etiquette of freedom. We can enjoy our humanity with its flashy brains . . . and take ourselves as no more and no less than another being in the Big Watershed. We can accept each other all as barefoot equals sleeping on the same ground. We can give up hoping to be eternal and quit fighting dirt. We can chase off mosquitoes and fence out varmints without hating them. No expectations, alert and sufficient, grateful and careful, generous and direct. A calm and clarity attend us in the moment we are wiping the grease off our hands between tasks and glancing up at the passing clouds. Another joy is finally sitting down to have coffee with a friend. The wild requires that we learn the terrain, and nod to all the plants and animals and birds, ford the streams and cross the ridges, and tell a good story when we get back home.

In stories, wildness is preserved.

Opposite page: *low water level in the swampy Delta.*

CREATURES OF THE DELTA

The Delta, like a long unfinished poem, is always undergoing revision. One example is a Mobile-Tensaw Delta Total Insect Bio-inventory Project (TIBP) which was established in the spring of 2000 to catalogue the Delta's insects. John W. McCreadie of the University of South Alabama Department of Biology is involved in mapping the biota of the Deltaic wilderness.

The scope of wilderness/wildness addresses more than the masked and anxious face of a raccoon or that of an otter, whose bold nose and whiskered face is more beguiling than his sleek-slim body and purposeful tail. The Delta is life. It is also death. It is the threat of mosquitoes, that though we would grant every living thing its space, have no consideration for bird or man, infecting them with the West Nile virus, or in earlier years, malaria and yellow fever—disease gone wild.

A Hank Ketcham "Dennis the Menace" cartoon features Dennis, his arms waving wildly in the air, explaining to a kid who is scared to sleep outside in a backyard tent that there aren't any *wild animals* about. "I know that," the little boy says. "Then what's the problem?" Dennis asks. "Mosquitoes," the kid answers. Dennis explains that he and his friend will be sleeping in a tent. The next frame shows Dennis and his friend standing on the steps of his house looking out at the distant tent. In the dark, overhead, there are bright yellow circles of light with a tiny bug in the center of each. Dennis and his friend stare, and with dawning amazement, the friend exclaims: "They got flashlights!"

MOSQUITOES

Although we may joke about mosquitoes, they are far from funny. They wiped out the town of Blakeley following yellow fever outbreaks in 1826 and 1828. The adventurer Trader Horn

might well have been speaking of the vanquished town when he said, "nothing in Nature is so full of solitude as a spot where man has been and gone again."

Mosquitoes breed in the sub-tropical, muggy, hot and humid Delta. It takes only seven days for the birth cycle to issue forth the wily fly as it goes from egg to larva to pupa to menace and scourge. Mosquitoes, a member of the Culicidae family, are of the order of two-winged, long-legged flies known as diptera. According to the American Mosquito Control Association, there are more than twenty-five thousand species of mosquitoes. *Anopheles* means hurtful, and it is the Anopheles mosquito that carries malaria. It belongs to the genus Aîdes, though the classifications of some mosquitoes are undergoing change.

Mosquitoes begin their life in the water. The sultry weather of the Mobile-Tensaw Delta furnishes a propitious environment where the female mosquito can thrive. She is the demon mosquito, the "blood-sucker." It is she who bites, not the male. Why? She needs protein to produce the eggs she deposits on water surfaces, on ponds and streams, but also on containers filled with water if someone may carelessly have left one behind. In about a week, the footless larvae (spelled with an "e," the word is plural; the singular designation is larva) will hatch and "wigglers" will lay claim to the Wild. Since the female mosquito can lay as many as four-hundred eggs, quite a number of "wigglers" skip along on top of the water. Most take in air through their breathing tube. The *Anopheles* lack a siphon and lie parallel to the surface of the water, getting their supply of oxygen through a breathing opening instead of a tube.

After the molting larva changes into pupa, a resting phase occurs. This does not mean, however, that the pupae are immo-

Left: *Tombstone in Blakeley bears silent witness to yellow fever epidemics of 1826 and 1828.* Opposite page: *nesting brown pelican with chick.*

In the Realm of Rivers

bile. They are quite active, and after sinking to the bottom of a water supply for a few days, their skin splits, and the adult mosquito begins to lead its tiny life. It spends a bit of time on the surface of the water where it dries out and then it is ready for flight. If naturalists assume that everything in nature should be granted its own space and the ability to lead its life, it is perhaps hard to fathom what the good of mosquitoes may be.

The mosquito was and is a deadly enemy almost impossible to wipe out, much less tame. James Becnel of the U.S. Agricultural Research Service says that "the idea of eradicating mosquitoes is not realistic." DDT was used to spray mosquitoes, but it proved to have a deleterious effect on the environment, killing birds and other insects.

The Brown Pelican

Legend has it that old fishermen never die; they just disappear awhile and come back another time as pelicans. There is, however, a problem with this story, especially if a consideration of DDT, banned in the United States since 1972, is factored into the equation. DDT kills pelicans, and thus the fisherman's future life would be at stake. High concentrations of DDT affect calcium metabolism and when it is found in the blood of brown pelicans, the birds' eggs become paper thin and consequently fewer pelicans are born.

Since the publication of Rachel Carson's book, *Silent Spring*, the use of pesticides has been a significant environmental issue. Chlorinated hydrocarbon was banned by the federal government in 1972, and since that time, the brown pelican fortunately is no longer on the endangered species list in Alabama and Florida.

Two characteristics distinguish the Brown Pelican. In contrast to the White Pelican (*Pelecanus erythrorhynchos*), known for its soaring and diving—sometimes as much as fifty feet—for its feast, brown pelicans are communal and gather together to

48

surround the fish that are scooped into their pouches.

The Brown Pelican is a magnificent bird, especially noted for its long flat bill and black wingtips. Poet Dixon Lanier Merritt's lines on the pelican are famous for pointing out that the bird's mouth can "hold more than his belly can."

Pelicans nest on beds of sticks, straw, and other collected debris along a waterfront. They usually pair up for a year to brood and raise their young, mostly between December and February. They are friendly creatures with low-sounding grunts that seem to say to fishermen: "We'll even take fish offered from human hands."

Tri-Colored (Louisiana) Heron

The Tri-Colored Heron's voice is startling, a series of *awk uuh uuh uuhs* that could be conceived as an expression of pain. It is a creaking or deep groaning sound, but mostly the Tri-Colored is silent except when startled or disturbed. Its feathers then become ruffled, the bird displays its grand boa, and the sound of *awk uuh uuh* can be heard, the gutteral caw syllables that are said to have a wideband frequency of some 200 to 1000 Hz.

The name "Louisiana Heron" is something of a misnomer, for the bird is also at home in the Mobile-Tensaw Delta. The Tri-colored female does not select her nesting place. This choice is left to the male of the species and he selects the site prior to mating. Egg-laying follows, usually in April and May when the female lays three or four splendid light bluish eggs about every other day. Both parents, then, take part in the process of incubation which lasts around twenty-one days. The nestlings begin to fly when they are about five weeks old.

With long, exquisitely thin, brown-yellow legs that correspond to their long limber S-shaped neck, the male and the female look generally alike with sharp, peering eyes and long pointed bill, although the female's bill turns blue during the time of breeding. Blue feathers cover most of the bird's body except for a chest and belly that bear white feathers. The white stripe that runs down the front of the bird's neck is a characteristic marking of the Tri-colored Heron.

Adult herons are twenty-five to thirty inches long. They are graceful in the water and delicately pick up their feet as they look for food. Sometimes the birds wade in belly-deep and when they see their lunch or dinner or breakfast, as the case may be, they are adept at grabbing fish, insects, and frogs. The word "freeze" seems applicable to their behavior, for if something startles them and they sense danger, they stand stark still and point their bills toward the sky. It is as if they think they can blend into the environment and not be seen as they don't, at once, take wing. The nesting sites of the Tri-Colors, threatened by human disturbance, are of concern, and their habitats need to be protected.

Snakes and Serpents

Some forty to sixty species and subspecies of snakes thrive in the Mobile-Tensaw Delta. Among the more deadly and poisonous snakes is the Diamondback rattlesnake. Although it is said that snakes won't bother a person who doesn't bother them, it would seem prudent to know a snakebite remedy or two. Some Native Americans adopted a remedy for snakebite that consisted of finding a black chicken, splitting it down the back and attaching it to the bite. When the chicken's skin turned green, it is said to have absorbed the poison. There are, however, not too many black chickens at hand to make this remedy very effective.

Other Delta snakes include the striped ribbon snake that is so rare it borders on extinction. The black racer, the poisonous and deadly coral snake, the hognose snake, pygmy rattlesnakes, and

Opposite page: *Tri-colored Heron.*

watersnakes of which there are several species: the *Aglistrodon, Farancia, Liodytes, Natrix,* and *Seminatrix* also find the Delta to be a happy home. The study of snakes is called herpetology.

Asked what rattlesnakes are good for, naturalist John Muir said that they were good for themselves, and that is all that is necessary. He says we need not begrudge them their share of life.

Snakes, however, are good for more than just taking up space and assuming their place in the grand scheme of things. They are good for science, good for literature, photography, art, and they are good for inspiration, for dreams. Nodding off before a fire in his study in 1864, Friedrich August Kekulé von Stradonitz had been puzzling over how he could account for the isomers of carbon compounds when he fell asleep and dreamed of Ouroboros, the snake devouring its own tail. When he awoke—as if by a flash of lightning—he spent the rest of the night working out the fact that the structure of benzene was a closed, hexagonal, six-membered ring. The snake of Kekulé's dream was a coachwhip racer or hoop snake, thus named because it rolls down hills at amazing speeds, coiled in a circle with its tail in its mouth.

Other allegories, stories, and fables of snakes have become ingrained into the culture. Two wands or staffs came to be associated with the medical profession. The wand of Aesclepius, the Greek god of medicine and healing, was a staff around which a single snake is entwined. In ancient times, nonpoisonous snakes were left overnight with the sick, a practice thought to promote healing.

The cadeusus, the staff of Hermes, the son of Zeus and Maia, goddess of plants and spring, is winged and has two snakes coiled around it. These snakes are associated with the intertwining of the masculine and feminine which, in the Yoga system are the feminine Ida and the masculine Pingala. This rod or scepter became associated with surgery and with healing that took place among humans in the physical world. It resembles the human skeleton, the spine with its attached nerves, arteries, and veins.

The snake in the Garden of Eden figures prominently in the Bible's book of Genesis and is part of the creation story. Pulitzer Prize-winning author E. O. Wilson says in *Biophilia* that "science and the humanities, biology and culture are bridged in a dramatic manner by the phenomenon of the serpent that is at once seductive and treacherous."

Writers, if not actual victims of ophidiophobia, are certainly fascinated with snakes. In addition to the snakes of mythology, the title of British poet and novelist D. H. Lawrence's book is *The Plumed Serpent.* It features Quetzalcoatl who bore a human head and symbolized death and resurrection. Another work that emphasizes the serpent is his poem, "Snake," that likens the creature to a "king in exile, uncrowned in the underworld, now due to be crowned again." To kill it is to "have something to expiate, a pettiness." The poet Emily Dickinson writes about "the narrow fellow in the grass" and says that she "never met this Fellow / Attended or alone / Without a tighter breathing / and Zero at the bone." According to legend, St. Patrick led the snakes out of Ireland when he prayed and fasted at Clew Bay, but the real reason there are no snakes in Ireland has to do with ecology. The land bridge that connected Ireland and Britain became submerged when ice melted during the last Ice Age and snakes were unable to slither their way into the Emerald Isle.

RATTLESNAKES

St. Patrick obviously did not set foot in the Mobile-Tensaw Delta, nor did the last meltdown of the Ice Age bring about their destruction, for whether or not snakes are to everyone's taste, they do show up at the dinner table. Some folks like to round them up to eat them. The rattlesnake can be skinned, cut into

Opposite page: *coiled diamondback rattler.*

In the Realm of Rivers

three or four inch pieces, rolled in a mixture of flour and corn meal, milk and egg, salted and peppered and deep fried in hot oil. Some say it is delicious, but a more elaborate dish for those with discerning taste is Rattlesnake Chili. It consists of a rattler six feet long that is skinned and boned and that supplies about a pound of meat.

This is added to a mix of onions, garlic, bacon, canned tomatoes, jalapeno peppers, kidney beans, black beans, pinto beans, a tablespoon each of cumin, oregano, and peanut butter. A half-cup of gold tequila can be added just before serving time, and it is said that this boosts the flavor. Served with grated cheddar cheese and a spoonful of sour cream, the dish is delectable. Such a fine repast, no doubt, is another thing a rattlesnake is good for.

Cottonmouth Moccasins

E. O. Wilson says that when he was a boy, he had a "secret ambition to find a 'Real Serpent,' a snake so fabulously large or otherwise different that it would exceed the bounds of imagination." His seeking such a serpent is a story of danger, mystery, and suspense. Young Edward came upon a cottonmouth moccasin that stared at him with a sort of "frozen half-smile" and eyed him with "yellow cat's eyes." Wilson describes his horrific adventure in *Biophilia*:

> I moved through the snake handler's routine: pressed the snake stick across the body in back of the head, rolled it forward to pin the head securely, brought one hand around to grasp the neck just behind the swelling masseteric muscles, dropped the stick to seize the body midway back with the other hand, and lifted the entire animal clear of the water . . . The moccasin, however, reacted in

Opposite page: *the dangerous cottonmouth water moccasin.*

a way that took me by surprise and put my life in immediate danger. Throwing its heavy body into convulsions, it twisted its head and neck slightly forward through my gripped fingers, stretched its mouth wide open to unfold the inch-long fangs and expose the dead-white inner lining in the intimidating "cottonmouth" display. A fetid musk from its anal glands filled the air. At that moment the morning heat became more noticeable, the episode turned manifestly frivolous, and at last I wondered why I should be in that place alone. Who would find me? The snake began to turn its head far enough to clamp its jaws on my hand. I was not very strong for my age and I was losing control. Without thinking I heaved the giant out into the brush and it thrashed frantically away, this time until it was out of sight and we were rid of each other.

Snakes figure in fiction about the Mobile-Tensaw Delta. In his book *Cottonmouth*, Mobile novelist, painter, sculptor, and originator of chants, Julian Lee Rayford, writes of "rattlers and black snakes and coachwhips, puff adders, blow snakes," and of coral snakes and their refulgent color. The cottonmouth, however, commands the title of Rayford's book. He describes the cottonmouth as "the most exotic snake known to man" and reports that "it lives in legend like an enchanter surrounded by a magic aura, in an emanation of fiendish reward for the temptation he offers."

The cottonmouth moccasin is a rather unexciting, somewhat ugly coppery brown snake. It is not very long, but Rayford says it is "thick and fat, like a short man with tremendous lunging shoulders."

Although Rayford's prologue, "Down By The Riverside," begins with a magnificent description of the swamps that lie along the "golden-red muddy-green-yellow river," it is the cottonmouth that claims two full pages of the novel. Like Edward

Above: *Non-poisonous banded water snake.*

Wilson, Rayford is fascinated with the snake's cottony mouth, and his description of it is riveting.

Rayford's snake "sits in the bright sunlight, and it opens its mouth. . . . That mouth is as white as a piece of cotton. So they call it Cottonmouth." The snake is a frightful "other," an alien that both attracts and repels. Someone comes upon it, Rayford writes, as it is:

> expanding its jaws to the sun, for all the world like a full-opened white bloom. . . .
>
> People have been known to go right up to that terrific bloom to pluck it, and when they did, God ha'mercy on their blundering, unperceiving souls, for it is a blossom of death.
>
> They say there is no serum for the bite of a cottonmouth. They try rattlesnake antivenom. . . . When he bites, he clutches with his fangs like a bulldog and holds on. But twists his body and flings himself over on his back, hanging tight until his hypodermic fangs are emptied of every drop of the deadliest juice of death in America.

E. O. Wilson says the cottonmouth possesses a terrible hatred of man. Rayford confirms this opinion. He says that "some punishing demon lives within him" and that with his head sticking up out of the water, "jabbing back and forth in tempestuous rage," the snake is "like a cantankerous old man who breaks up a ball game and screams lividly at the kids that he will bring down all the vengeance of the law upon them. That's the cottonmouth."

Adult water moccasins are generally twenty inches to four feet inches long. Baby cottonmouths average around ten to thirteen inches. As they grow to maturity, they change color from copper to a dark brown that appears almost black. Their heads are flat on top, and it seems as if the creatures like to show them off. They gape and display the white lining of their mouths. Bill Finch, in a July 20, 2001, article in the *Mobile Register*, says the cottonmouth floats higher in the water than nonpoisonous snakes that tend to keep their bodies submerged except for a portion of their heads, but he says that people shouldn't judge a snake by the way it rides a river or stream. Considering the accounts of Edward Wilson, Julian Rayford, and Bill Finch, one might easily discern that caution would be advisable before swimming in Delta waters, no matter how inviting a river or stream may be.

Snakes feast on fish, frogs, lizards, and other snakes though they won't turn down occasional repasts of small turtles, salamanders, baby alligators, or small birds. They don't eat people, but for those who confess their ophidiophobia, it is a good thing indeed to stay out of their way.

THE PYGMY RATTLESNAKE

Edward Wilson's penchant for snakes did not diminish, even after he was bitten by a pygmy rattlesnake. This encounter, described in both *Naturalist* and *Biophilia* obviously made an impression on the youngest Boy Scout counselor at Camp Pushmataha near Citronelle, Alabama.

That sound in the woods? Well, it isn't a bee buzzing. It isn't a mosquito whining. It's a pygmy—watch out! The snake may be small, but its rattles are meaningful and shouldn't be ignored. Pygmy rattlesnakes have mean dispositions; they are aggressive, and Wilson says that they don't hesitate to strike.

It is fortunate that the pygmy rattlesnake, seldom longer than eighteen inches, is less poisonous than the diamondback and canebrake rattlesnakes. Nevertheless, Wilson's account shows that its bite can harm. Bitten by one as a boy, he nursed a swollen left arm and index finger for several days but suffered no permanent damage, he says, except for "a fingertip that grows a bit numb at the onset of cold weather."

The pygmy rattlesnake bears black splotches along its dusky gray, reddish-orange, or tan body. It has a long reddish-orange stripe that extends from its back to its head.

The pygmy is at home in the swamp and hovers around streams and ponds, slithers in among the pine flatwoods, and feasts upon small creatures like mice and frogs. Because it is small, it may not be as easily spotted as a diamondback rattlesnake, but it is to be heeded nevertheless.

THE CORAL SNAKE

The deadly coral snake is often confused with the scarlet kingsnake, so anyone walking in the woods would do well to learn the difference between the two snakes. A mnemonic comes in handy: "If the head is black, look out Jack," or "Red next to yellow will kill a fellow."

Experts may be able to tell at a glance the placement of the colored bands on both the coral and scarlet kingsnake and they may realize that the coral snake isn't as temperamental as the anxious pygmy, but a novice strolling through the wood would do well to forget the saying "red next to yellow will kill a fellow" and swiftly get out of either snake's way.

SNAKES ARE NOT STRANGERS to the Mobile-Tensaw Delta, so it is not surprising that there are many stories about them, and once even a legislative act. The Alabama Legislative Act 45 of October 31, 1950 states that

> [any] person who displays, handles, exhibits, or uses any poisonous or dangerous snake or reptile . . . to endanger the life or health of another shall be guilty of a felony, and upon conviction shall be imprisoned for a term to be fixed by the court of not less that one, nor more than five years.

The crime was reduced from a felony to a misdemeanor in 1953, but a snake-wielding terrorist still could have been fined and sentenced to up to six months in jail. Although these acts are no longer on the record books in Alabama, there is a reckless endangerment law that says a person may not menace another by physical action that creates "fear of imminent serious physical injury." Fascination with snakes can only be carried so far. ✏

Below: the hog nose snake flares its neck (inset photo) like a cobra when it feels threatened. Opposite page: ribbon snake.

A Boy Named Scout, Rattlesnake Talk, and a Six-Pack of Water

TWO south Alabama boys just turned fourteen and on the cusp of manhood agreed to test their prowess by spending a night alone deep in the Mobile-Tensaw Delta where black bears are said to roam and one of the most dangerous snakes in the world, the Eastern Diamondback Rattlesnake, is sometimes seven feet long.

"Bet you won't last an hour in the swamp, Scout," Sport said. He was proud that he was three months older than his friend, even though he weighed four pounds less and was an inch and a half shorter.

"Those snakes lie so still, you don't know they're near you," Sport said. "It's noisy, too. All kinds of sounds. Owls hooting. Coons half grunting and half barking. A snake'll be all coiled up, and it will have its fangs in you before you know it. I won't tell you what will become of you after that. So you go first, you're always telling me you're the smartest."

"Sure," Scout said.

And just as the sun was waking up, Scout set out on his venture. Harold, his Papa's friend, had agreed to boat him across the river from Hubbard's Landing and deposit him on the opposite shore.

"Here, boy, eat up," Harold said, handing Scout a couple of biscuits loaded with hog. "You'll be fishing for your supper, and you'll hafta get your own bait. No rod and reel, kid—just this pole," he said as he chucked it in the boat. "And, oh, here's a six-pack of water."

"Thanks," Scout said. He was excited and ready for adventure. "I'm going to get me a rattlesnake taller than I am," he told Sport, who had come along for the ride across the river and who was sitting in the new double ender that Harold had recently built. He was glad this morning that he wasn't going first.

"You gonna have to swim back," Sport hollered. He'd been told by his Uncle Leslie about hollering on the water. YOW EEE EEE, he screamed, and his voice must have carried a mile. He hollered again. YOW EEE EEE. He hollered so loud he wanted everyone back at Hubbard's Landing to hear him. He wanted them to hear him all the way back to the Stagecoach Restaurant where the Chief of the Alabama State Lands Division was having coffee.

"Go for it!" Harold told the boy. "Don't listen to Sport. I'll pick you up in the morning, right here by these old cypress knees."

A Delta camping scene.

"Yes, I mean, yes sir," Scout said. He was a born and bred Alabamian, and he knew his manners. His mama would bless him out if he didn't say *sir*. "Yes sir," he said again.

At first Scout thought the woods were the most fantastic thing he'd ever experienced. He saw butterflies, a wild turkey he wished he could take back for his mama to bake for dinner even if it weren't yet Thanksgiving. He could smell the bird roasting and almost taste the spicy stuffing inside. It upset him though to think of old "Tom" stuffed on the dining room table. The bird ought to be out there in the woods, wild and free to find a mate. It was sad that something so good to eat had to be slaughtered.

His mama's cousins, James and Jason, who came over every other Thanksgiving from Tampa, Florida, were vegetarians. Maybe they were on to something. Scout thought about it, but decided to postpone that decision until he was in college and off on his own. It would upset his Ma if he didn't eat up and praise the food. Since he'd turned fourteen, he'd even started giving the blessing.

For a moment Scout thought he saw a yellow bat, but it wouldn't be hovering around in the daytime. Sport's Uncle Leslie had told him bats were valuable because they ate the mosquitoes.

He said some people from Auburn were studying bats, putting little radios on them to see what they were up to. It would be fun to be a biologist, Scout thought. Maybe a botanist. He'd learn all about wildflowers. His pa had told him that the oak leaf hydrangea, a flower native to Alabama, had been described by William Bartram some 225 years ago. He'd written a paper in his science class about how it was Alabama's official state wildflower and gotten an "A," and his teacher had written, "Fine job. Isn't nature the bee's knees?" She had underlined "the bee's knees" and had written "ha ha" in the margin.

IT WAS GETTING HOT, the sun was high overhead, so Scout took off his shirt and started fanning himself. It was like being in another world here among the pond scroggin. A piliated woodpecker was pecking away near the top of a tall pine, and Scout marveled at the bird's colors. He whistled, but the woodpecker went on pecking like the boy made no difference whatsoever to the wilderness. Scout was the stranger here.

Looking down at his feet, Scout saw a huge locust. It was so long it seemed to reach from the tip of his index finger to his wrist. Scout bent down to look at it more closely, but the insect never moved.

"Aren't used to anybody bothering you, huh? I bet with those legs, you can hop a sight higher than I can." Scout sat down on a fallen log and decided to have a biscuit and some of his water. The sky overhead was as blue as his mama's eyes, he thought, but not near about as pretty.

Time passed as was its wont, and Scout was so busy that he hardly noticed that daylight was moving toward dusk. It was then he thought about preparing for the night. "Hmmm," he said. "Wonder where to settle." He started looking around for leaves, and just as he reached down to gather a hand full, he saw a snake with yellow diamonds on its back. A rusty red stripe ran down its spine. It was coiled up, and its tongue was flickering out of its mouth. Scout jumped back. He couldn't seem to catch his breath he was so frightened. It seemed like his legs would buckle under him, and he couldn't even run.

"Whatcha doing whippersnapper?" the snake said, turning his head first in one direction and then the other.

"What?" Scout answered. Maybe the sun had fried his brain. He was hearing things.

"Said, how you doing?" the snake replied. "Got a favor to ask."

Scout backed up and put more distance between himself and the rattler. It was stretching out now, and Scout could see that the serpent was at least five feet long.

"Come closer," it said. "I've been hankering to go to a zoo. If I can just get to a fancy zoo, I can slither around and show myself off. People will come and admire me. I haven't found many tasty rodents or birds to eat of late, and I'm getting old. Near about fifteen," the snake said. "Bet I'm older than you are, boy."

THE SNAKE SEEMED FRIENDLY. It seemed to smile, and Scout, it could be said, was beginning to lose that innate fear of snakes that the naturalist E. O. Wilson wrote about. Scout had read his book *In Search of Nature* as his summer reading project. There was a whole chapter devoted to the serpent. He'd learned that the scorpion goddess Selket was called "the mother of serpents."

"Come, pick me up," the snake begged, softly and sweetly. Scout had learned that most snakes really didn't hiss.

"Promise you won't bite me?" Scout asked.

"Promise," the snake said, moving the tip of its tail ever so gently.

"Better not," Scout said. "You seem friendly enough, but I know your nature. Once a snake, always a snake." It was one of his mama's favorite expressions.

THE SNAKE BEGAN TO RATTLE. He began to coil up again, and his head was moving menacingly. He didn't seem so friendly now, and he struck out at the boy. Scout had found his legs, and he was running like he'd get an Olympic gold medal. He didn't look back. When he was far enough away and there was no way the snake could be seen, not even in the distance, Scout stopped and drank a whole bottle of water. Mr. Harold and Sport won't believe this, he thought.

In preparation for settling down for the night, Scout decided he wouldn't bother gathering leaves. He found a clearing, built a fire, and before it died down to ashes, he fell asleep. He was tired, and the last thing he remembered was the full moon. It was bright overhead. In fact, it seemed to light up the wildwood in the most beautiful way he'd ever seen. He could see a magnolia and close to it an elm and sycamore. He started counting the magnolia's leaves and before he got to a hundred, he fell asleep.

Scout didn't wake up all night, but in the morning he was hungry, grabbed his pole, caught himself a worm and began to fish. Nothing was biting and he thought about the bacon and scrambled eggs his mama would have fixed him for breakfast. He was ready to go home, and he hoped it wouldn't be long before Mr. Harold would be coming to get him. High in the top of a nearby tree, an eagle looked down with his sharp eye and was ready to catch some fish. Scout was proud of himself. He'd spent the whole night in the swamp, and he began to sing, "Shake, rattle, and roll. Shake, rattle, and roll." He'd be one up on Sport now. It would be his turn for a night alone in the wildwood.

Across the river, Mr. Harold's double ender was getting nearer and nearer, and Scout began to holler: IIIIIII DIDDDDD FINEEEEE.

"I did fine, Mr. Harold," the boy said as he jumped in the boat.

"Where's your snake, son? Thought you'd get you a big one."

"Well, I saw him," Scout said. "In fact, believe it or not, we had a conversation. He wanted me to pick him up and carry him off to a zoo."

Mr. Harold chuckled. "That's a good one," he said, patting Scout on the back. "That's a good one all right."

MORAL 1: You better know what something is before you pick it up. Moral 2: Boys reared in south Alabama aren't fooled by a snake in the grass. ༄

Longevity

Trees do not count their age as people do
or complain of time's passing.
Their longevity is a matter of heart;
rings that mark the years
are secret and hidden inside.

Trees never ask a river how old it may be.
They sway to the song the wind sings
and bow, in reverence, to the rhythm
of ripples, for that is answer enough.

Trees know how things unseen—
like taproots—reach down, touch darkness,
grow and gather strength
to support the length
of tenacious trunks
and arms that reach out in celebration.

What Does Wildness Mean?

Gary Snyder investigates the meaning of *wild*,
how it gathers into itself everything free
and asks what we do with such definitions.
The wilderness is mystery and mellow dark;
it is dawnlight and rain, thunder,
storms and hurricane winds. *Wild*
is the gator's wide mouth opening;
it is frogs and snakes swimming
murky waters or seeking shoreline shelter.

Those who wag their human tongues
refer to the Mobile-Tensaw Delta
as the Swamp. They say the word
with awe and love, with a voice
as reverent as rain when it has been dry
too long. *Wild* is the second largest estuary
in the United States, the long tongue of rivers
with lovely mouths. It is a refreshing taste.

The word *wild* is the aroma of a startled skunk
wearing his white mantle of hair like a shawl.
Except for the scent, he might be somebody's pet,
male or female, free to roam until settling down
on the velvet cushion of night.

Wild is a red-bellied turtle struggling
to keep his home upon his back,
his tooth-like cusps hanging
from the side of upper jaws
protesting extinction.
Wild is the slither of snake

(mind, most do not hiss as humans do).
It is a fire ant's boastful queen,
a cricket talking in the night,
the cry of peepers
peep peeping by a pond
when the sun
goes down.

Wild is more than a definition
to memorize, something learned at school:
the Old Norse *villr,* the pre-Teutonic
wilthijaz that conjures up the sound of a trumpet
playing during an evening's visit to Preservation Hall,
Satchmo and New Orleans, that wild town,
those wild rhythm, swamp tours and Marie Leveau
stirring snakes and toads in a savory stew.

Is there place in classrooms
across the USA for *wild*
to situate itself—as in John Milton's
"Warble his native wood-notes wild"?
Or is it the thoughts of John Pilgrim
who contrasted the wild wood world
of earthiness with heaven as he walked
through the wilderness of this earth?

Or can it be that what is wild in each of us
desires to come home again to the place
where the caw of the crow
and the croak of the frog
define the word
on a discerning tongue:
wild, wilderness, woman,
Earth, Mother, Delta-land.

The lonely skunk, or polecat.

As One Shall See in a Summer's Day

In the sweet scent of honeysuckle summer,
flies hatch on bayous,
mosquitoes whine. The males
drink nectar from daffodils;
the females seek birds to bite.
The smell of bream beds
cause cautious noses
to twitch. Bullfrogs hrump,
bass strike waiting hooks,
and deer watch
in successful sunlight
the irreducible day.

Beyond Translation

Say *cielo, ciel, suty–*
spirit and breath.
Speak sky and add whatever cumulus means
in any tongue. Add the stretch
of a stream's blue meandering. Find
solace in the movement of marsh,
in the reach of trees
looking into water
as it releases reflections.

Delta run wide;
know that nature has answers
beyond translation.

Granted Bearings

Asleep in her den
with new-born cubs
suckling, spring
cuckolds winter
in ways humanity
fails to understand.

In the den where Bear hibernates
sleep begins to lose its claim.
She stirs and wakes
to forage for food, to find
insects riffling rotten logs,
to savor sweet honeycombs,
but her forte is finding fish
in the fullness of earth's awakening.

The Mobile-Tensaw Delta
is sacred common ground,
a wilderness of shared necessity
whose promise lies in being preserved.

Warm in Winter

Secure that the Delta
is where he ought to be,
Bear sleeps warm in winter.
The world at ice-point,
is no concern of his.

From his perch in a tree-fork,
he watches spring
brim and stir,
eyes the lily drink April rain
and watches for a man
whose footsteps
threaten extinction.

Bobcat

As quick as the click
of a camera, a bobcat
with stubby, white-tipped tail,
leaps upon a mouse, a rabbit, turkey,
or squirrel, revels in a feast,
but eats no more than three pounds
of meat unless it can be hidden away
to nibble until the scat is duly rotten.

It is easy to forget
that such an expressive face,
such agility and grace
hide a hunter's intent.
An aggressive cat
bent on getting its prey,
also teases and likes to play,
grabbing a smaller bog frog
that will serve for a meal
if the "bob" feels its belly
growling, unfulfilled.
Stub-tailed cats prowl at night
on padded feet and pull in their claws
to creep ever so quietly in the swamp,

placing their hind feet right where their fore
feet have been to lessen the snap
of twigs and silence noise.

In spring, in April or May,
a mother finds a safe den
under fallen logs or in a mass of root
beneath a fallen tree where she can give
birth to kittens who are blind
for the first ten days
of their lives, but then
follow mother into sunlight.
She twitches her tail, and they prance
behind her, investigate a weasel who
dares them to come her way.
Papa cat sidles off. He does not stay
to help mom teach the babies
all they should know
and show them how scent-marks
will lead them home, until,
as ceremony and custom show,
it is time for freedom,
time to roam alone
and live within the five
to fifty miles that will be
their new-claimed territory.

Deer-Foot Haiku

The scrapbook of earth:
the press of a deer's fleet foot
near a fallen leaf.

Masterpiece

So much beauty breaks the heart—
deer-heart, poised on the edge of oblivion.
Does the wind wrestle with anxious trees,
with the stir of leaves
on display in the Delta where you stand,
alert and questioning?

Is man scent strong in dry altered air?
Do your eyes warn of misdirection?
Should you flee? The wholeness
of your body, the round, brown eyes,
uplifting head drawn in natural perfection,
bear witness to fall.

I have seen your antlers,
mere decoration, in human dens.
I have walked upon your skin—
the rug under faltering feet.
You are a feast in times of famine,
the treasure of a hunt.

What is it we must conceal
when we ask what it means
to be human
or animal
in this time
of inexplicable need?

Lineage of a Delta Bullfrog

With the richness of time
distinct in his throat,
the bullfrog sounds summer nights
and conveys the Delta's daily news.
He has called for a wife,
and their lineage will be a line
of frogs eight inches long.

He declares that dorsal green
is the finest color for a frog,
but croaks about cousins
who are drably brown
and about some
who are dusty gray.

Rana catesbeiana
is on his tongue,
the savory of supper:
an unwary mouse,
a tiny bird, a serving
of insects. He has a hearty
appetite and will live,
he thinks,
to the fortuitous age
of forty.

Alabama's official State Reptile—the red-bellied turtle.

Pseudemys Alabamensis

His house boasts a ruby-red door,
but don't come knocking.
He won't stick his head out.
This real estate is not for sale.

A Grasshopper Sonnet Song

Whether the most impressive K-k-k Katydid
Pterophylla camelliofolio
or *Scudderia furcata,* who's also
known as the green Fork-tailed Bush Katydid,
receives an answer to its mating call,
they are a green study, but can you say

in what special and particular way
they differ? What characteristics all
grasshoppers share? They habit Delta marsh
and are at home in the wood. They have hind-
legs that are quite incredible. You'll find
the Southeastern Lubber's smell is quite harsh
if disturbed. And you question how they sing?
They make a viola, rub wing on wing.

A Matter of Repetition

The owl asks who
is mocking whom?
He thinks he's wise,
but isn't able to discern
when the mocker's faking.
Perhaps it's Fats Domino
crooning "On Blueberry Hill."

Or is it John Craton's composition
for the young violinist practicing
pizzicatos, glissandos,
and trills? Native Americans
called the mockingbird
"one with four hundred tongues,"
and it seems that all of them
are loose at once if the nesting

bird of the Mimidae family
is stirred to fury.

In the Mobile-Tensaw Delta,
when the world is moonstruck
over music warbling the night,
no bird, not even one of the human kind,
need ask who or question
the rightness of a song.
It is enough to join in
and sing along,
sing along, sing along
as if the mockingbird
knows more than enough
about wooing
and loving.

White Head, Dark Body, Watchful Eyes

Above the body of land
that is the Delta,
above Chocolatta Bay,
the brown feathered body
of the bald eagle,
nests in an eyrie of sticks.
With eyes as open as the sky,
this far-sighted seer
of south Alabama—
the *haliaeetus leucocephalus*
scans the water, watches
a mullet jump, and with ready talons
seizes it in a hundred mile an hour dive.

Some bald but lordly birds like this
live for fifty years it is said,
and when they wed
in aerial flight, in sky-dancing clasp
of claw, they are mates
for life.

A man and his wife
should habit so and soar
as high in bold reciprocity
within the encircling
horizon and the commerce
of the grand and animate earth.

More Than a Bird's Eye View of Poetry

A balladromic bald eagle
lights on the branch of a live oak
in Nenemoosha Bayou
in the thick green of a delta-summer.
A gator with eager shuttered eyes
lounges on a log just birled
by a waterman. She has children
nestled on her head; they bask
in the suant sunlight.
It is in such wilderness as this
that the black bear used to roam
before the scent of fear, of extinction
brought him to seek another home.
The red-bellied turtle wears a sensor
under his skin. Those who steal him
will rack the consequences
of their robbery.

How soon will human kind
make themselves extinct?

White powdered poison posted
through U.S. mail created
certain commotion and confusion;
it is man and not the wilderness
jargogling the land.
Code orange flashes across
TV screens all over the USA.
Warnings of smallpox
and leprosy, of germs
of indeterminate shape and size
are more than threats, are possibility.

What can save us is poetry.
William Carlos Williams said people
die everyday for lack of what is found
in it, in sonnets, villanelles, odes,
free verse, love poems, and the making
of metaphors for peace, all in the holy name
of survival.

Sulphur Butterflies

Fairy sulphur butterflies
with light, bright flamboyant yellow wings
record in petals of perfection
moments
of bliss
found
in
the sanctuary
and
treasure trove
of
a single sinless flower.

Opposite: *butterfly-adorned cardinal flower.*

Breath, Wind: The Miracle of What Happens

The Mobile-Tensaw Delta knows war-wind,
knows what happens when
the voice of thunder comes loud
from the sky and the Breathmaker
blows and blows, threatens and blows
and the pine bends low, almost as low
as the earth, and its needled hair
falls loose on the footpath and the hickory
snaps and is broken and the oak tries
to stand against whorls unseen
but felt in limb-wrenching dislocation—
the ineffable, destroyer and redeemer
scattering tiny seeds, bearing them
into a wildwood wilderness
where they wait for tomorrow's sunrise
and the warm moist nurturing mud-ground,
primer of life for otter and owl, bobcat
and beetle, spider and fern and butterfly,
heron lifting one thin leg from settled water,
Dawn Man and Woman, Blue-Sky Woman
and Twilight Man, never ending breath of life:
all Creation.

IN THE REALM OF RIVERS

Owl Eyes

From their perch where trees
revel in dancing,
on the bend and twist and lean
of subtle limbs, owls watch
as night squeezes
color from the fade and fall of day.

They repeat only one question:
who? who? who?
There may be a rustling
in the grass, perhaps
a responding hoot,
but without expectation
of an answer.

In breathless air
presence
lies gathered in congregations
of kite and mottled duck,
osprey and sparrow,
cottonwood and pondweed:
all together,
all in their accustomed place.
Let it be.

First Light

In that quivering moment when night
is reluctant to give way to dawn,
to the weight of the earth
still heavy with sleep,
the eye of the sun, yellow
and whole, sees the shape
of what is to come,
sees tomorrow and yesterday
as one and understands
the heart of the Delta
is revealed in first light.

It Is As If

in reading
first one paragraph
and then another,
rivulets of line
upon lingering line
and there and then
from time to time
a period, a stone, a pebble,
a full stop.

How do we read the river?
It is as if words run together;
it is as if we cannot read
through the thick of water
the things we ought to know.

Perhaps we want too much,
expect to drown sorrow
by diving into depths,
to rise without understanding
mornings and evenings
flow into each other
and come to expression
in a single solitary slavering mouth

that speaks of treading
as a means of finding
prayer and song
as a means of finding
that the shore is nearer
nearer than dreamed
while the river goes on
as ever, goes on, goes on.

Often Unaware

We know her breath,
her sighs and fits of storm;
we know the way light came
and she gave us life,
this good earth, our mother.

We know the stirring
of her limbs—oak and ash,
elm and magnolia
and the way our own faltering
arms stretch, reach, and bend
under stars,
those bright flowers
budding in the night.

We have heard the bald eagle twitter,
the crow caw. We are habitants
together, the wild that is in them,
the wild within us—hide and fur,
rib and bone,
roots and berries
that sustain bodies
often unaware of the need
for preservation.

The Gathering

Everything
should be allowed to be
what it is, where it is,
in its place,
casting a shadow,
depending
on the light, the multicolored
shades of sky
gathering
in family reunion.

Following Your Trail

(An Address to William Bartram)

You speak of fusty ferruginous rocks
that encumber the heights of hills
along Mobile Bay,1778, that day
you arrived at Taensa—the smell
of dampness, of age and mold
clinging to stones you hold
in your hand. Cemented with iron oxide,
the sandstone is rust-red. Dust colors
the fingers with which you write
pinus taeda, nyssa sylvatica,
quercus rubra, fagus,
while visitors follow your light canoe
220 years after you voyaged
the river, mapping the flora
and giving it a name.

In this new millennium,
would a spy glass and lexicon suffice
those who wished to see
what you saw in pebbles and stones,
in high cliffs, in the rills and meanders
of this native land?

You say the air is humid and still,
scarce a breeze in the sultry
sticky, mosquito-ridden July.
The sky, stricken with thunder,
protests, perhaps, the invasion
of loggers yet to come,

the way they bore a hole
in the loblolly's heart
and pull a plug. But you,
Will, marvel at the pistillate
flowers, the pale shades of green,
pink and purple-red depending
on the stage of development.
The pine, you note, is not alone;
it stands along side the *nyssa sylvatica*—
the blackgum and common red oak
from which warblers call,
the red-cockaded woodpecker,
the osprey and bald eagle
seeking nest along 16 miles
of the marshy river
that extends from Hubbard's
to Live Oak Landing. The cypress,
ash, sycamore, yellow poplar,
as well as pine, that line
the waterway are the tallest,
straightest, most enormous trees
you've ever seen. The cane
grows thirty, maybe forty
feet tall, taller, by far, than a woman
or a man, but not as tall as their pride
in the Mobile-Tensaw Delta land
as they walk in naturalist shoes
and follow your path
along the Bartram Trail.

The Nature of Psalm

Standing on the bank of the Apalachee River
watching crows take to the sky,
it is possible to imagine
having wings; it is possible
to see the marsh
as a shawl wrapped
around a waist waiting
adornment. The moss,
its uncombed hair
never in need of styling
brushes against the Delta's
fulsome brow.

Standing on the shore of Chuckfee Bay,
it is possible to forget
calibrations, calculations,
clocks and watches,
computers, cell phones,
any sort of chronometer,
but yet know continuence
and think of how the heart

keeps its own steady and purposeful beat.

Standing on the bank of Bayou Tallapoosa,
it is possible to believe
how the sound of wind
in cypress crowns
are prevailing psalms,
chanted celebrations
of a sheened and sheening earth
singing supplejack and muscadine,
willow and wisteria,
ibis and sparrow,
singing salamander and bass,
eagle and otter,
and the human being, *like to a tree*
planted by water-rivers
in season yields fruit
and the leaf never withers
as all who join in communion
give thanks,
give thanks.

Shades of Blue

Drawn in freehand by Nature,
there is never a need for erasure.
Every thin line etched in white
and yellow forms a splendid blend of light:
purple, violet, the essence of blue
intermingled with the greenest hue
of long narrowed leaves curving,
and arching in summer's wind, deserving
notice, this tall bold Iris whose name
rainbow, gives nod to beauty and acclaim.

Loose on the Tongues of Trees: A Lesson in Survival

Standing tall on the edge of tomorrow,
roundly facing it,
the same as yesterday,
spring stirs in the lullaby of limbs,
each reaching toward music the sky knows
in bursts of blue, considerations of grey,
the joisting of comely clouds.

Recitations of magnolia,
scribed ivory petals of perfume,
are ready at hand,
are invitations to take this magic
as bees do in scent-searching pleasures.

Words on the tongue of trees
are etched in its rings
as old as the world is

in its rightness. We learn
our place standing
in breathless brooks,
in forest glens,
in moonlit meadows,
in fields of plenty.

We learn roundness,
even in our lumbering,
how the future and the past
are really the same,
as we stand resilient to storms
the rootedness
of our lives teaching us
that being bent
is not the same
as being broken.

Opposite page: the Alabama champion cypress, deep in the Mobile-Tensaw Delta. Photographer Dennis Holt was guided to the tree by Mike Thompson, left, and Clyde Eurick. Overleaf: the tree's size is hard to believe. It towers over the surrounding forest.

Lily A-Bed

What sundry summer slithery things
sprawl in sleep beneath
coverlets of lily green
when night comes on
in the Delta? Do they dream
of what they will do
when the sun rises
or wonder how
they will pass
the day in gainful employment?

The stream has a well-dressed bed.

Mushroom Caps

Such haberdashery is not for sale
for any price: the smooth white cap
with brown-trimmed under-rim
of the Meadow Mushroom, *Agaricus campestris,*
the fan-shaped, grayish brown, edging round
in concentric circles, the pretty pileus
of the Artist's Fungus, *Ganoderma applanatum,*
found on broadleaf trees, living or dead.

And there, on connifer stumps or logs,
the Witches Butter, *Dacrymyces palmatus,*
with it lobed gelatinous heady brain,
fain needs added adornment to compliment
its yellow-orange, orange-yellow crown.

A bishop's miter boasts no more grandeur
than that worn by the Old-Man-of-the-Woods,
Strobilomyces confusus, standing under an oak.

Forget the fedora, the sombrero,
the deerstalker on the heavy head
of Sherlock Holmes. Dismiss
the trilby, keppi, balaclava,
porkpie, helmet, or mortarboard,
walk in the wild and admire
the Shaggy Mane, *Coprinus comatus,*
the light brown, bell-shaped curly cap
on the stalk of an Inky Cap family member.
The Stinkhorn family of Ravenels
merit acclaim. The Mushroom's cap
brooks no imitation.

In the Realm of Rivers

A Place To Be Found

In forests of pine,
oak or ash,
where deer eyes
and eagle eyes
burn in the night,
where the heat of day,
makes a body retreat
and gulls, too hot to laugh,
light upon a limb and pause
in flight, there is shade
and a place to rest.

In the heart of a tree,
as in the heart of a woman,
the core of a man, there is a
place

to withdraw, a sanctuary,
a haven in which to hide
when thunder claps
with its seventy-odd fingers,
seven thumbs, and a tempest
of grief. The forest shows
how strong and solid
roots can be.

In the heart of a tree,
beneath limbs
proud of their intricate beauty,
the art of branching out,
there is a place for stillness,
a place to hide
and to be found.

Opposite: *fledgling barn owls.*

A Lesson in Navigation

The river
doesn't worry
about 10:00 o'clock,
about income tax,
cholesterol,
or
senatorial elections.
Its concerns are deeper,
much deeper.

Rivulets
in eternal cycles
of meditation
give those who look
into the water's mirrored depth
a self
they never knew.

Talk About Pigging Out at the Stagecoach

Annie says Albert's a Bear;
he says she's a dear to say so,
but George is singularly chicken.

George says he's tired of being
everybody's goat. The problem is
Jim's a snake in the grass,
and never to be trusted.
Have to keep an eagle-eye
on him and look out.

"George is a bird-brain;
don't pay attention to him,"
Jim says.

"Maybe, hoss." George snarls,
"but I'm not sly
like a fox and can be trusted."

Everybody eating burgers
and pigging out
at the Stagecoach joins
in the discussion.
"George is a hawk," they say,
"No way's his brain small.
He even joined a book club,

read Ed Wilson's *Naturalist,*
and Lynn Hastie on Red Eagle."
He meets with a coffee group
every week to talk about
animal rights and problems
of pollution. If nobody
wants to listen to the conversation
at hand, they can just bug off.

George confesses he may not know
which tails wags what dog sometimes,
but he won't be badgered by yellow dog
democrats, oversized elephants
or out of state dissenters.

Lennie pulls his chair up to the table,
leans back on two thin legs
trying not to fall backward
and states emphatically
that residing in the Delta
is living high on the hog,
for no matter what anybody
has to say about it,
life is wild. Just wild,
and there's nothing quite like
piggin' out at the Stagecoach.

A Walk Through Blakeley State Park

Trees in tardigrade motion
enjoy the quidnunc of evening rain
and bear testimony to peace
not known where city buses fume the air,
where planes land and take off and land
and people hurry about,
counting hours, minutes, seconds,
too busy to reckon the majesty
of trees in their splendor,
their veins, bountiful, moist,
tilting in the morning breeze:
sugarberry, *celtis laevigata,*
of the elm family, its twigs
slender and reddish brown,
lateral buds tight, appressed
and triangular in shape.

Walk through Blakely State Park
when the traffic of day is too busy,
too mobile and cars horns bleat and blow.
Marvel how trees take time in stride,
how they know when to stretch and rustle,
when to berry and blossom,
their leaves bowing, waving,
happy where they are,
and patient as humanity can seldom be.

Liquidamber's an exquisite word.
Say it, say sweetgum, too,
but look at the family name:
Witch-hazel. It spreads with age
as human's do, but is more upright.

Its leaves are stars with yellow lobes,
scarlet, orange, and purple. It knows
how to dress.

The landscape of the Mobile-Tensaw Delta
is but a lengthy chapter on leaves,
the button bush, *cephalanthus,*
bald-cypress, *taxodium distichum,*
persimmon, *diospyros virgiana,*
iovercup oak, *quercus lyrata*
of the beech family; its simple leaf,
oblong in shape with variable margin,
and five to nine lobes with irregular sinuses
that never sneeze.

Pastors should preach sermons on trees, tell the way
they suffer rain and thunder, bear up to lightening
when it flashes bright against the foreboding dark,
yet trembling in the lovely thrust of dapatical dawn.
What cordial refreshment is offered in woods,
these words on the tongue:
swamp tupelo, *nyssa biflora,*
water hickory, *carya aquitica,*
bluestem palmetto, *sabal minor,*
swamp dogwood, *cornus stricta.*

The sun touches avid walkers' shoulders,
warms in swirls of light.
If only this peace, these woods,
this small moment of forever
could beg forgiveness for hacking
and burning, there would be no war.

Section of the boardwalk in Blakeley State Park.

Looking for Light: A Story of the Fort Mims Massacre

SANTO could feel the sky's dark grief. He thought it was holding back the morning as he waited for the call of the hawk. Concealed by reeds and canes, hiding in a ravine, only three hundred yards from the fort he would attack, the young warrior listened. He was impatient. Why was it taking so long, the whistle, its high pitched *keeeeer, keeeeer, keeeeer* and descending scream that would send the Red Sticks into battle? Nothing stirred in the wind, stirred the silence, nothing that is, but the sweet twittering squeak of a humming-bird. It made him nervous. Vicey McGirth, once his foster mother, had told him as a boy that the hummers were his dead ancestors. "The ruby-throated bird should never be harmed," she said. "Once," she explained, "people lived in an underground world and everything was darkness. The hummingbird was sent to the wide world above to look for light. It flew and flew, up and up until it found a sky-path that led to sunlight, to the bright upper world where people lived.

Vicey's favorite story reminded Santo of his boyhood. He remembered the time the smiling woman with white, sweet-smelling skin had found him on her doorstep, afraid and begging for food. She had let him in, invited him to eat at her table, and adopted him into her family. He had been an orphan and had nowhere to call home. "You're just a little hummer," she would say, telling him again and again how, once-upon-a-time, a little boy as coppery-brown as he, with broad shoulders and blue eyes, was left alone while his parents searched the forest for food. The boy had a whistle he had fashioned from the bone of a deer, and he blew it and blew and blew, calling for his parents' return. In despair, he tossed his whistle into the air, and with astonishment, watched it come to life and turn into a hummingbird.

When the boy found his parents, killed by a bear, he had nowhere to go. The bird came each day and brought him an ear of corn. The hummingbird became the boy's companion and friend. He would call to it, and it would come, calling back "Chip chip, chip chip," and beating its wings thousands of times a second. One day it flew to the middle of the earth and asked the god of fertility to bless the Creeks' land along the Alabama river and make it fertile. "Rain came and corn grew tall on its slender stalks," Vicey said as she wrapped her arms around her foundling. "And little Indian boys never went hungry again."

ON LONG WINTER EVENINGS when Vicey's husband was away hunting, she would gather Santo, her son James, and all seven daughters around her for story time. They would sing songs, and each child, in turn, would tell of what had happened that made them glad or sad. Once Vicey chastised Santo for selling wasp nests. "Insects have as much right to their space as people have to theirs," she said. "No wonder the wasps were

angry over your meddling." One of the Halls from a nearby plantation had told Santo that he would pay him a penny for every wasp nest he could collect and bring to him, but if the nest contained so much as one dead wasp, he would not be paid.

Santo loved to boast of his bravery. He was proud that he had learned to endure wasp stings without crying. He was proud that he knew more about wasps than almost anyone in the Delta, and when his turn came to speak of his bravery, he would tell again and again of going into the woods to find wasp nests hiding beneath the loose bark of trees. He would tell how the wasps clustered together and explain that they did this to protect themselves. "When they get after you, whole bunches of them,"

Santo said, "you run like you've never run before. Like wind getting stirred up." The children loved Santo's story best of all.

The sun was beginning to rise, and still there was no whistle call. Santo could smell bacon being cooked at the fort. It made him hungry. He thought of the breakfasts he had eaten at Vicey's table and shuddered. He would rather be eating biscuits, sopping them in cane syrup, than going to war. He was afraid that the McGirth children and their mother might be inside the fort. Earlier last evening, as the threat of battle loomed ever near, Santo had slipped through the wilderness and found that the plantation of Zachariah McGirth was empty. He had watched as Zachariah slipped out of Fort Mims on his way to Boatyard on the lake. It was likely that Vicey, young James, and his seven sisters were staying at the fort.

Santo reached up and wiped his brow and picked at the paint smeared beneath his eyes. The horrible streaks of red and black seemed tight on his cheeks. He looked down at his body, almost surprised at its colored fierceness. He was naked except for the girdle drawn around his waist and the single cow's tail that hung nearly to the ground. His legs were muscular and strong, but they smarted from the needle scratches that extended from his thighs to his ankles as part of the preparation for battle. Santo had learned that one sign of bravery was to endure mortification of the flesh. Sometimes warriors even hacked at their own legs to make them bleed. They were proud that they could suffer pain and deny the hurt.

Santo frowned. It was too late to turn back. If he deserted the Creeks, his chosen people since he had left the McGirth household some years before, he would be called a traitor and killed. If he tried to return to the family who reared him during his boyhood, he would be shunned and mistrusted. He would have to stay and wait for war to begin. "Be careful what you choose," Zachariah had told him following the incident with the bees. "Once you choose a path, it's hard to stray from it, even when your feet would like to fly."

SANTO HAD KNOWN for days that the fever pitch of war was building. The inhabitants of towns such as Hoithle Walle, Fooschehatche, Cooloome, Sauwanogee, Talisi, Auttossee and others had taken to heart the war oath of the prophet Francis. His message sounded again in Santo's ears. It gathered in hovering clouds and echoed in the wind: "We have tried to be friends with our neighbors," Francis said, "and they have been ungrateful, taking our land, hunting our animals, and now, they kill our people." The prophet's heart burned with revenge. He urged the Creeks to war. "You must be ready to risk your life to revenge the blood of your kindred," he said.

Santo had stood in line to swallow the "black drink" that would purge his body before battle. He had not yet earned a war-title, and he knew that he was expected to prove his manhood. The White Man had, after all, invited war. The great chief, Red Eagle, said so himself. He said, "No red man can ever live in the white man's world." Santo reminded himself that this was, after all, why he had left Vicey McGirth and her family and gone to live again among the Creeks who were his mother's kin.

Suddenly the *keeeeer keeeeer* scream of the hawk sounded the alarm. A thousand warriors in full war paint arose as one from the troubled earth and rushed across the potato field toward the east gate of Fort Mims. It could not be closed due to the sand that had washed against it. Peter McQueen, the son of James McQueen and a Talisi woman, raised his fist in the sky, urging the Red Sticks to enter the gate. "Go," he shouted. "Go!" Those behind him took up the call. "Go, go!"

Major Beasley, who was in charge of the fort, had for days denied the report that Indians were near, but now he heard the war whoops, rushed out of his house, and ran toward the gate to close it. His efforts were of no avail. Warriors rushed through the entrance, and as they passed by Beasley, some shouting "Hoithlewaule, Hoithlewaule," the Indian word for "war," they knocked him to the ground, and beat him with painted war clubs.

Beasley called for help, but his own men were as ill-prepared as he. "Save the fort. Save the women and children," he shouted. Within moments, his voice was stilled. It was too late to save Fort Mims and all the people who would soon lose their lives. Blood flowed above the tops of shoes, and the initial thrust of battle lasted more than three hours. With the exception of one block house, every building was burned to the ground. Only twenty-two people escaped. One was a black woman named Hester who paddled a dugout all the way to Fort Stoddard to tell General Claiborne of the most brutal massacre in American history.

SOMETIMES, WHEN THE CALL of hawk can be heard in the stillness of the Delta, people say it is Santo's voice, clear and chill, that can be heard in the wind. They say that it is his shadow, cast in the light of the moon, that creeps across the Delta's floor. It is strong and yet strangely beautiful. Death is not part of its intonations. Rather it speaks of life and tells and retells the story of Vicey and her children who hovered in the fort in the thick of Indian attack. Maybe it is thunder, but those who have learned the ways of the wilderness say it is Santo himself, his voice ragged with time's passage, describing the death of his white brother, James and the sight of his mother and sisters struck dumb in the corner of a cabin. Thrumb. Thrumb. The door had just been broken in, and there with tomahawk raised, one of Santos's fellow warriors is poised to strike. With no time to think, Santo shouts "Halt. These detestable white wretches are more hateful to me than any others here. I have an old account to settle. Leave! There are other victims for you. Leave this family to me." The Indian with his fist in the air hesitates a moment, lets out the war cry, then turns and leaves the cabin. Santo says he will strike and kill even his kin if they rob him of his right to revenge. He looks in his mother's eyes. She is crying, her hand over her mouth, and Santo knows she understands he has come to save her.

When those who sought to kill the McGirths retreat, Santo, his voice no longer savage and loud, speaks softly. "Mother," he says. "Mother, come with me." Believing that the rescue was really a part of Santo's plan for revenge, the other Indians leave him alone as he leads Vicey and the children past the heaps of mutilated corpses and out into green and peaceful woods beyond the fort. When the family is no longer in danger, the brave warrior stands aside and reaches out his hand as he moves his mother into the shelter of his own hut. Here she remained with her children until it was safe for them to travel to Mobile and be united with Zachariah, who had thought them dead.

THIS IS THE POINT where the story of Santo is interrupted— for it is not just his story; it belongs to everyone who hears it and who in turn passes it on. The Fort Mims Massacre may have occurred long ago on that fated 20th day of August, 1830, but the story of Santo lives in legend.

The story of war is one that transcends time, and its destruction can only be redeemed in the selfless act of a Santo who risks his own life to save that of another he loves. Words, like tiny seeds, scatter in the wind, ride far in the beak of a hummingbird, or travel on the wings of a wasp before they take root in the soil of a common earth. A cloud passes over. There is the fall of rain. The book of nature, of the wild, of frail and faltering human nature, is told again and yet again, and it is in and through this telling that children today grow to maturity and that humans are united. Stories bring them together. Sometimes they save them from themselves. Otherwise war is irredeemable. ✐

Dandelion silhouetted in the sun. Opposite: *green-backed heron.*

IN THE REALM OF RIVERS

Brown pelican chicks.
Opposite page: mother
pelican with chicks in nest.

Cypress trees and knees in Chacaloochee Bay. Opposite: an old growth Bald Cypress tree and its reflection in the dark waters of Briar Lake.

View of the Whiskey Ditch area in the open marsh, between Chacaloochee Bay and the Apalachee River. This is one area where alligators have been known to build their nest and lay eggs in the spring. Inset: a newly hatched six-inch long alligator sunning on its mother's head.

Mushrooms near Byrnes Lake, after the area was flooded for weeks. **Opposite:** *lovely and historic Stockton United Methodist Church is one example of man's occupation of the Delta.*

Leslie Smith paddling one of his home-built double-enders in the Delta.

III.

Telling Stories: The Living Landscape

THE Delta is a storied landscape. It lives in the minds and hearts of those who have lived within its terrain and speak the ecology of its language, a common coexistence of dialect, slang, the vernaculars of geology and geography, history—indeed, telling words. The Delta's tongue utters not only the lisp of marsh wind but the fleet trail of a running deer in a mastery of human translation. Tom Gause says that the swamp isn't as big as it used to be, and we would never know how it was were it not for the stories that keep the past present, make the history and science and culture of the Delta an ever-living thing.

The Nobel Prize-winning novelist William Faulkner said that "the past is never dead. It's not even past." Poet and naturalist Gary Snyder writes:

> It is this present time, the twelve thousand or so years since the ice age and the twelve thousand or so years yet to come, that is our little territory. We will be judged or judge ourselves by how we dwell with each other and the world during these two decamillennia. If we are here for any good purpose at all (other than collating texts, running rivers, and learning the stars), I suspect it is to entertain the rest of nature. . . . All the little critters creep in close to listen when human beings are in a good mood and willing to play some tunes.

Robert Leslie Smith

"Swamp Rat" and Master Storyteller

LESLIE Smith, the son of Robert Augustus Smith and the grandson of Jesse Smith, Jr., says that by the time he was ten years old, he begged to accompany his father as he traveled to his logging operations. He was called a "Swamp Rat" by his peers. Born in the Delta in 1918, he still lives in the family home that was built in 1915. Home, the Delta, is where his heart is.

Smith served in the U.S. Navy, became a teacher, and taught at several schools in Baldwin County before becoming principal of Foley High School and subsequently the Baldwin County Superintendent of Education. He not only knows the area's rich and fascinating history, he contributes to it, builds his own double-ender, and has written a collection of as yet unpublished memoirs that make the Delta come alive and thrive with the vibrancy of his recollections. Anyone lucky enough to meet Smith at the Stagecoach Cafe for the Friday morning "Coffee Club" might prevail upon the venerable historian to show off his incredible collection of antique cars. They are housed in sheds behind his home and so "spiffed up" and shiny that putting out a finger to touch one seems a transgression. The Smith collection of antique autos is, no doubt, one of the finest that can be found.

An encyclopedia of historical information, Smith describes the changes since families living in the Mobile-Tensaw Delta in north Baldwin Country made their living from the land. "In the 1800s, everyone had to go to the swamp to make a living; there wasn't enough food or fertilizer, not even enough to take care of the animals." On up to the end of World War II, Smith says, "people sowed seeds in the earth, harvested wild animals for food and skins, grazed their domestic animals on wild grass, cut virgin timber and transported its products to downstream markets. People were at the mercy of seasons, weather and chance."

The story of the Delta is one of shared experiences. It's about oxen and the men who drove them, about night rafting and camp life, about the practice of hollering and pullboating, not to mention a host of logging and sawmill tales handed down through generations.

"Every logging operation could chronicle trees falling on people," Smith says, reminiscing about the days when men and mules did the work instead of tractors and machines. "Mechanization came late to the logging business," he says. "There used to be drownings in the swamp. It was a dangerous place. There was illness, too. Everybody had malaria, and they used to treat it with 'quinin,' a concoction called 666 that was a mix of quinine, water, and alcohol." Atabrine (quinacrine hydrochloride), Smith says, replaced quinine in the area when Japan occupied the far East and cut off the supply of cinchona bark from which quinine is derived. Atabrine was extensively used in the South Pacific in World War II, and atabrine pills were available in saucers set on the dining table at mealtimes. "Everyone turned a dull yellow color," he adds.

SMITH REPORTS that there weren't many doctors around Stockton, but he remembers in particular Dr. Malachai Coghlan who used to go out in his horse and buggy and make house calls. "He didn't talk like anybody else. Used to precede everything with 'Zeee.' He'd say, 'Zeee, I think it's true' and 'Zeee' this and that. His Creole-architecture house was built in 1912."

Perhaps it is the teacher in his blood, but Smith makes history come alive. "Did you know," he says, "that Andrew Jackson and his family spent time in north Baldwin County?" He chuckles as if that fact itself is as "wild" as the area's woodlands. "Yes, his wife spent two years in Tensaw country, but she complained about it and didn't like it at all."

Smith explains that the Creek Indian War was a civil war. Those who adopted the white man's way fought those who did not. "My fifth grade teacher, Mr. Till, owned the land that is the site of Fort Mims." All of the Delta's history, it seems, is situated in Leslie Smith's brain, every story, every tidbit of history, slouched back and comfortable in an easy chair waiting for a moment of rediscovery.

Smith describes a swamp dweller's life on the banks of the Alabama River. He explains that a house would be raised ten feet or so above the ground, above the high water mark on nearby trees. "Two medium trees," he reports, "are selected to support two diagonal corners. Two mulberry posts form the other two corners of the approximately sixteen-foot structure. Sills are spiked to the trees and posts, and as I recall, there are no other braces. The walls are weathered, sawed pine boards. The roof is part rusted metal and part six-foot split white oak shakes. A ladder leads up to the door of the one room structure."

"Imagine this," Smith says. "Cooking is done on a small wood stove set out under a tree. There is a roof of shakes over the stove. Nails are driven into posts and utensils hang from them. Nearby there's a corn crib, and not far off, there's a double-ender tied to a willow tree on the river bank."

Lunch in the South and in and around "the swamp" wouldn't be lunch without a healthy serving of collard greens. In fact history books attest to the fact that Southern children didn't suffer from rickets or malnutrition during the World War because greens were a diet staple. Mothers used to put the juice from the boiled collards or turnips into babies' bottles and give it to them to drink. This "pot liquor" was full of good vitamins and minerals. Smith tells how swamp collards were grown upside down. There was an arbor-like construction situated about ten feet from the family house. "Four mulberry posts were set in a square of about twelve to fifteen feet," he says. "A branch was cut to form a Y, and into the Y, there was a strong runner and poles laid across for rafters. Across the rafters was a thick layer of brush and on top of that at least a foot of dirt. Chickens ran about on top of this structure and collards hung upside down." Smith says he doesn't know why collards weren't planted on top, but he says that farmer and timberman Charles Earle, a man he referred to as "Mr. Charlie," used to say the chickens and a hog or two would go up there when the water got high and floods came." Smith says he couldn't see how chickens could coexist with a hungry hog.

OTHER STORIES OF LIFE in the Delta involve Mr. Charlie and his logging operations. Mr. Charlie's contractors would search out small, perfect ash trees, cut them, and drag them to the river bank where they would be rolled into the river and put on a raft to be picked up by a tugboat. "Green ash logs float like a cork," Smith explains. "Mr. Charlie never took water with him on his forays into the wilderness. He didn't drink swamp water and didn't take along any food. His practice was to

Wild turkeys are common throughout the Delta.

go at midday to the homes of swamp dwellers and ask if someone could fix him a chicken or maybe a corn cake."

"Soul food" may not have been invented in the Delta, but the food is certainly *soul* and folks say it's as good as it gets and maybe better. The Swamp used to abound in crawfish and catfish. "Swamp dwellers," Smith says, "kept a box built of white oak strips with a ready supply of catfish that would be used not only for fine dining, but for sale or barter and also as feed for hogs." Chickens on the roam, or perched atop a collard house, would find their necks wrung and their legs served up as drumsticks. The Missus of the family would sashay out into the yard, grab her a chicken, all plump and sassy, and wring its neck around until the hen quit protesting about it. Then she'd scald it, pluck out the feathers, and fry it up. Then it's just a matter of time before that chicken will find itself in a satisfied swamper's stomach. The diner will lean back, smack his lips and start thinking about maybe one more helping. "Chicken was breaded with corn meal, rather than flour in those days," Smith says. "People rarely had flour. They would just make their way to the grist mill when meal ran low, and though life in the swamp was hard and dangerous, no one went hungry. There were dried peas that had been threshed by beating in sacks, and there were cushaws, that ovoid-shaped squash with green, warty rind that could be kept all winter. Rabbits, too. They often appeared on supper tables. They were killed by knocking them off a floating chunk during high water and salting them in barrels for summer use. Loggerhead turtles were caught on catfish limb lines and butchered by chopping them open with an axe. Nope, nobody went hungry." In Leslie Smith's lexicon, food and memory are an ultimate dish, and they go together like chicken and dumplings, another dish frequenting the dinner table. Of course, in the South, 'dinner' was the meal served at noon. Supper was served at five or six o'clock.

Smith says that a piney woods logging camp was always located near a flowing spring, for the first business at hand in pitching camp was to find a source of water. He explains that a strainer would be placed in a three-foot deep hole and driven the rest of the way to the water table, perhaps ten feet in all. A pitcher pump was threaded on top, water from a mud hole was poured in for prime, and the well would soon be in place. After about ten minutes of pumping, fresh water was ready for drinking—even if it tasted and smelled of decayed vegetation.

THE LOGGING CAMPS housed men in tents, but if the camp were to be used for an extended period of time, lumber would be laid on the ground for a floor and a tent pitched over the top. Outdoor tables were used in fair weather. On weekends, the camp cook would ring a bell hanging around an ox's neck when it was time to eat. A typical breakfast, according to Smith, would consist of "grits, fried salt pork, tomato gravy, flour bread—which we now refer to as biscuits—molasses and coffee." Each man would sweeten a quart of water with a cup of molasses, tuck it into a rucksack slung over his shoulder, and sip on it through-out the day. Smith laughs and says the molasses water was the forerunner of Gatorade.

If men worked close to the campsite, they would come in around noon for their dinner of beans, cornbread, fried salt pork, and duff. "Duff," he explains, "was prepared from flour, sugar, and condensed milk. It was loaded with dried peaches or apples and baked as a cobbler." If the men were beyond the proximity of the camp, dinner would be taken to them in molasses buckets.

At supper, rice, mixed with "mack'el fish" would be served with tomato gravy. This would replace the noontime beans, and accompany fried catfish or wild "hog" if the boss had been able to kill one. Smith says that "the real difficulty of feeding a camp crew lay in the transportation of raw material that had to be delivered to a camp site. Sacks stacked on fenders and running boards and back seats of open cars would have to be loaded in a boat and paddled for miles." Storage was crude and poorly protected from the elements.

"Sometimes," Smith says, "camp dwellers would be served 'Damfudont.' 'What's that?' a wary, but hungry, man would ask. 'If you don't eat it to-day,' the cook replied, 'then damn if you don't eat it tomorrow!'"

CAMP STEW WAS ANOTHER DISH especially relished by the loggers, and Smith provides a recipe in *Gone to the Swamp*, a collection of memoirs: "Buy ¼ lb of boneless stew meat per man. Put a small amount of lard in the bottom of the stew pot. Stir fry until most of the meat is seared. Add water and simmer. Season with salt, black pepper, and onion.

Plan on at least a three hour cooking time. If in doubt, cook longer. You can't overcook. At about the halfway point add thickening made from flour browned in a skillet with water added. Serve over rice. If using squirrels," he adds, "cook and serve bones and all. Be sure to have at least half a squirrel to a man. More is better."

Smith says that the backbreaking work in the Delta took its toll. Men were killed by felled trees that crashed where they were not supposed to, and there were also epidemics of yellow fever and malaria.

One of the engaging stories Smith tells of life in the Delta is that of Violet Boston who lived on the edge of the Alabama River swamp. He prefaces his

story by recalling the custom of addressing older African Americans as "Aunt" or "Uncle" and explains that the terms were "a mark of respect for age."

He says the route to Robert Augustus Smith's camp was right past the front door of Aunt Violet's house. Because the road was so poor and it was impossible to get to the lake by truck, it was necessary to travel on foot for the last lap of the journey. "Now, Aunt Violet was well up in age, and though her back was stooped and she was a bit feeble, she still raised a garden of collards and such behind a fence made of sticks and brush woven into a barrier so thick it would keep out any wandering livestock. It was so thick, I doubt a rabbit could get in."

Aunt Violet's voice was not weak at all, nor were her ears hard

Rabbit nest.

of hearing. When she heard men passing near her house, she would come out on the front porch and begin to pray so loud her words had no trouble traveling to Heaven. "Oh, Lord," she would cry, "I ain't got no flour! Ain't had no flour in a long time! Please, Lord, send me some flour! A little bit! Just a little bit is all I ask."

Smith says that if there were any flour in the sacks the men were carrying, there would be less by the time they had passed Aunt Violet Boston's. "And it wouldn't be long," he said, "before she was heard giving thanks: 'Thank you, Lord, thank you. Thank you. I'm gonna fix me some flour bread now.'"

Later, when the boats, loaded with trees, were on their way to the mill, "Aunt Violet could be heard calling again. 'Oh, Lord, I ain't got no shoes!' She'd lament that she was as barefoot as when she came into the world and would complain about how cold her feet were. 'Just a little money,' she would wail. 'Lord! Lord, please send me some shoes.' A man who might be passing with an extra coin or two would leave it outside Aunt Violet's gate. And again, she would cry: 'Thank you Lord. Thank you for sending me money for shoes.'"

Sometimes, Smith, said, Aunt Violet would cry out for coffee, but it seems that she received whatever she asked for, a mark, perhaps, of her indomitable faith.

SMITH SPEAKS, TOO, of bears and trees. He says that a few hundred yards west of the west bank of Bottle Creek, there was a huge pine tree growing in the center of the Delta. "Since a pine tree cannot live in an environment where it is covered by flood waters for more than a short time," Smith writes in his memoirs, "the very existence of the tree is a mystery. Yet, covering its bark from about four feet up the trunk to about ten feet, are the healed scars of vertical slashes on all sides of the tree." Smith says that legend has it the marks were made by bears.

"When a male bear enters a new territory, he seeks out the local *bear tree*, rears on his hind feet and slashes the bark with the claws of his forefeet. If his mark is higher than others, he stays. If he cannot reach the highest mark, he travels on. Fast!"

THE OLD VERNACULAR of the Delta is less familiar in the region than it used to be. Smith, who has built a double-ender, explains the difference in it and a pirogue. "A double-ender is a boat with a sharp bow and stern that was used to transport men and supplies around the streams and rivers. It was especially useful in traveling through flooded woods. The widest part of the double-ender was about one-third of the way from the bow."

Paddling a double-ender is, in itself, quite a proposition. "One person." Smith says, "sits on the rear seat and paddles from one side. If someone wants to paddle from the right side, it is necessary to grasp the top of the paddle with the left hand and the shaft of the paddle just about the blade with the right hand." The back, he explains, needs to be straight, the waist bent at just the right angle so the boat can be kept straight. If passengers are along and help paddle, Smith says all paddles must enter the water at the same time, without a splash. A paddle should never scrape the side of the boat.

Smith says that the best wood for building a double-ender is juniper because it is light, yet strong and durable. Next choice is heart cypress and then pine, though Smith says poplar is acceptable. He says that anyone with carpentry tools can build a double-ender and that the job takes only a few hours. That may be true for such a veteran boat builder as Leslie Smith.

A bum boat, used to push and pulls logs in ponds and streams near a saw mill, was a craft with blunt ends. It was a utility craft and the term was said to have derived from "boom boat," that operates inside a log boom.

ANOTHER BOAT was a two-pontoon craft called the gunboat. It was designed to transport to market wood that was so dense that the logs couldn't be floated down the river. Smith says he doesn't know why these boats were called "gunboats." He thinks they might have been used to support heavy guns that once attacked enemy forts. The gunboats, Smith explains, were the property of sawmill owners, and they were loaned at no charge to loggers if they sold their product to the gunboat owner.

"The Delta today has become a playground," Smith says. He particularly laments the fact that the art of hollering is all but lost. "Men," he says, "used to communicate across surprisingly great distances by whooping, shouting, crying, or yelling. Tyroleans yodled, American Indians gave war whoops, and Confederate soldiers gave the unnerving rebel yell, but people in the Delta simply *hollered*, often for the sheer joy of hollering."

Smith explains that a proper holler could be heard a mile and a half if part of the holler was over a lake or a river. "Everybody knew everybody's holler," he says. Though folks could be heard hollering on their way home from work, Smith says that the very best time for hollering was "just before sun-up when an owl was likely to holler back at you."

Smith says that every man and boy developed his own special style of hollering, and it was as distinctive as a signature. Smith writes in his memoirs about how plowboys would holler to say "Good Morning" to each other. Lev Munnerlyn, who sometimes rode in Robert Augustus Smith's Model T, would holler "AH-OO-AH-UH-HOO-O-O. Boog Seals would let out a much shorter "YAH-HAR-R-R." Smith says that Wash Knott, who was too old to work, would sit on the front steps of his place and holler to say "I'm still here this morning." Smith's father would answer with his own "HEE-HOO-O-O."

Leslie Smith's mother, formerly Sue Bryars, was quite a hollerer, too. Smith remembers her hollering out "LES-LIE-E-E-E-E-E" or "GOR-DIE-E-E-E-E-E" when calling her boys home.

"I don't remember why hollering stopped," Smith says, "but it stopped for me when World War II began. I never heard hollering after the war. Maybe it was because everyone's way of life had changed. A man is not likely to stop his tractor to holler so the boss man will know he's on his way to the barn. The noisy tractor will tell him that. He is not likely to stop and holler so his wife will know when to put supper on the table. He can just blow the horn on his pickup. And besides," he adds, with something of sadness present in his voice: "Who has time to say good morning to the whole neighborhood these days?"

YET WHEN SOMEONE RINGS Smith's door bell, he often hollers from the comfortable chair where he is watching television and one is fortunate indeed to hear his "YAY-HO-O-O!" Meeting Leslie Smith is an unforgettable experience. And in those moments as reverent as history, as memory, of days when "Gone to the Swamp" was a familiar cry, Smith says there are times when he can hear his mother calling her father. "PA-OO-O-O-O! PA-OO-O-O-O! PA-OO-O-O-O," she hollers. And he can hear her father answering "YAY-HO-O-O-O! YAY-HO-O-O-O." Smith says that he finds himself answering the door with the same holler his maternal grandfather used, keeping the past present and the swamp stories ever alive. ✑

Opposite: River otter.

MARVIN BRYANT

Protecting the Bald Cypress

THE Bald Cypress *(Taxodium distichum)* with its protruding, knobby knees, is one of the more familiar trees in the swampland of the Mobile-Tensaw Delta and one of the easiest to identify. Perhaps the single largest tree recorded in the Alabama Forestry record books is that of a cypress which is a whopping 131 feet in height and 27 feet in width. Located near Lower Bryant's Landing on the property that belonged to George Edward Bryant, Jr., and his brothers Marvin and Robert Bryant, it has been said that the lumber from this tree alone would build a large house.

Marvin Bryant, who was once a Baldwin County minister, reported that his grandfather thought about cutting the old cypress tree and using it for stock flats to transport livestock down the river. His father, however, had no intention of cutting that tree. It was one of a kind, and folks who came to see it marveled at its stature. "Take a few fellows to wrap their arms about that one," they said.

Marvin Bryant, who was photographed with the old tree, said that his father showed it to him when he was just a boy. Then he'd forgotten about it until Harry Still of Bay Minette found it again some twenty-five years later. This was in 1989, and some thirty people in six boats made their way into to the swamp near Bayou Jessemine to place a marker at the base of the tree, claiming that it was the largest Bald Cypress in the USA.

It is said that the Bald Cypress got its name because the wind came along and sheered the trees tops and left behind rounded and pointy heads, but it is the knees that garner the most attention. In fact, one version of the Cajun "Twelve Days of Christmas" grants six cypress knees for the true love's present:

> On dem sixth day of Christmas,
> my true love she gave to me:
> Six cypress knees,
> Five poules d'eau,
> Four pousse café,
> Three stuffed shrimp,
> Two voodoo dolls,
> And a crawfish in a fig tree.

The beautiful reddish-brown wood of the Bald Cypress is a prize gift; it is durable and fine-grained, disease resistant and excellent for construction. The lady of our poem may know a thing or two, know that a man's home is his castle, especially if he can build it with wood from cypress trees. ❧

The distinctive knees of the Bald Cypress. The giant cypress discussed opposite by Marvin Bryant is pictured on pages 108–109.

Brothers Jimmy and Harold Bryars.

IN THE REALM OF RIVERS

The Baldwin County Hunting Club

Just Call Him "Nameless"

STORIES are handed down and passed around like cornbread, filling soul and stomach alike. Leslie Smith lends an account that he says is associated with the legendary Baldwin County Hunting Club in its early days. He says the story comes from James (Jimmy) Arthur Bryars III, who helped to manage the club hunts in the 1930s. The following tale, told to Smith by Bryars, is reprinted here from Leslie Smith's unpublished "Gone to the Swamp."

It is a perfect example of how stories are told and retold until they become living history. The hero of the story, Smith says, shall be nameless to protect the innocent.

Nameless was a Stockton, Alabama, boy, probably sixteen years of age, who liked to hunt. He had mastered the art of being a "stander" and aspired to be a "driver." Standers were placed along trails at numbered stands (small signs tacked to trees) out of gunshot of each other. They were forbidden to move more than a short distance. This limitation was for their safety and that of the next stander. They awaited the chance to shoot a deer that might be pursued by dogs or frightened their way by the shouts of the drivers. The drivers, much fewer in number, were free to move through the whole swamp. Indeed, they were expected to cover the whole area in an agreed pattern, whooping, imitating the barking of dogs, thrashing the brush, and seeking innovative ways to frighten deer. It was their duty to enter the thickest briar patches, wade the ponds, and go through areas a prudent bear might avoid. Only the most athletic, woods-wise and stout of

wind and limb could meet the responsibilities of being a driver. Drivers must know the lay of the land, the location of the stands, and favorite hiding places of wary bucks. The penalty for not knowing these things was to risk being shot by an overeager stander and becoming lost on a cloudy day. It was not for the old, the very young, or the inexperienced. Their rewards were increased chances of having a shot at a choice buck and the admiration and respect of fellow hunters. Drivers generated almost as much respect among fellow hunters as watermen among fellow loggers. Nameless had a burning desire to become a driver!

HIS CHANCE CAME ONE DAY when the hunt for the day was laid in the area from Bear Creek on the east, to Knapp Lake on the west. Jimmy Bryars, the hunt master of the day, gave instructions. He explained the lay of the land and loaned Nameless his own compass. "Now, drive generally north. You will eventually come to a line of standers. Keep the lake on your left and the creek on your right. If you get lost, go due east until you hit Bear Creek. Follow it south and you will come right back here."

Nameless struck out in a northerly direction making the prescribed noises. He was not seen or heard from by his fellow hunters that day or that night or for much of the next day. A search for him began about mid-afternoon and continued until dark. Again at daybreak it was resumed and continued until mid-afternoon when word was brought into the woods that Nameless had called his parents' home in Stockton from Mount Vernon, Alabama, on the west side of the Mobile River, miles from the scene of the hunt. A team was dispatched by boat to get him.

NAMELESS WAS UNHURT by the experience and his love of the sport was not diminished. The next day he appeared right back on the hunt. He did, however, have to face an interrogation by his fellow hunters, who had expended so much effort searching for him. Jimmy Bryars, hunt master, bearer of the most responsibility, remembers that the questioning went approximately thus:

"Well, what happened to you?"

"I got lost."

"How did you get lost?"

"I don't know."

"How did you get on the other side of the Mobile River?"

"In a boat."

"Whose boat?"

"Some hunters."

"What hunters?"

"I don't know, just some hunters."

"Were they some of our hunters?"

"No."

"How did you get with them?"

"I waved them down."

"From the bank?"

"Yes."

"They took you across the river to Mount Vernon?"

"Yes."

"You called your parents from there?"

"Yes."

"Why didn't you go east to Bear Creek like I told you?"

"I didn't know which was east."

"Didn't you have a compass?"

"Yes."

"Where is my compass now?"

"I threw it away."

"Why did you throw my compass away?"

"Because it was broke."

"What do you mean it was broke? What was broken about it?"

"Well, it just wouldn't point but one way."

Jimmy is sympathetic to anyone who finds himself in Nameless's situation. He says that he has himself experienced disorientation in the swamp when his every instinct told him one thing and his compass told him another. He points out that it takes sheer willpower to follow the needle when one's mind and body tell him to go another way. ↩

Duck hunters in the Delta.

Tom Gause

Loving Life in "the Swamp"

Sitting in his home in Stockton on an early August morning, Tom Gause blends science and culture when talking about the Mobile-Tensaw Delta. "Folks who grew up and live in the Mobile-Tensaw Delta call it 'The Swamp,'" he says. "It's a vital part of history in this part of the county." He defines the Delta as the area that extends from Satsuma, Creola, and McIntosh on the west to Boatyard, Fort Mims, and Tensaw on the east, and down to Polecat Bay, Chacaloochee Bay, Apalachee and Blakeley rivers, and to Bridge-head. "There is a fault line along Highway 43," he explains. "On this side of the river, there is a graben [a slippage in the earth bounded by faults]."

Whether at home or at the coffee club that meets regularly at the Stagecoach Cafe, Gause talks with contagious excitement about life in the swamp that he loves. Those unfamiliar with the ways of the woods occasionally have to say, "Whoa. Slow down just a bit," so they can catch up with what he means when he speaks of logging in the Delta, of watermen and gunboats, and of spike poles and billies, which are a collection of small logs bound together, a sort of small raft.

"Timber was an economic resource in the swamp since day one. Do you know about float roads? Floating started in the late summer or early fall of the year. A crew would go into the swamp

Opposite: Tom Gause calling on a cow horn.

and deaden the timber." Gause explains that years ago, trees were huge. They were cut down and left until they dried out. Before chain saws, axes and cross-cut saws were used to cut timber. Heavy axes were heard all through the woods, and lighter-weight axes were for use on the water.

Then the watermen came along and floated out the logs when the river flooded. "Let me tell you," Gause continues, as a slight smile lights his face, "the watermen were impressive. They stand on the rolling logs and dance them from stump to float road. Watermen are as agile as dancers."

High water usually occurred sometime between January and early spring, and float roads that were cleared of debris were cut to be thirty to forty feet wide.

There is an art and a science to high-water logging that relates to the flooding of the Delta. Gause explains that timber that floats well—such as cypress, ash, cottonwood and tupelo gum—is felled in the fall when the swamp is dry enough to go in, de-limb the logs that float, and gather up the the non-floaters to be loaded under "gunboats."

The waterman carries a long straight spike that is anywhere from fourteen to sixteen feet long, with a hook on the end. "There is a band along the bottom," Gause explains, and with the pole, the waterman can push against trees as well as push on the bottom of the trail that leads down to the float road. The hook propels the waterman. When he breaks into the float road itself, he'll be picked up by a double-ender [a wooden boat] and be ready to make his way back into the swamp to start another round. "There's a sense of pride in being a waterman," Gause says. "It means you know how to endure being wet and cold and face the possibility of falling in the river. If the waterman's lucky, he'll get plucked out of the water, brought to shore, and dried out by a warm fire. A waterman makes good money for his work, but he earns it."

THE DELTA WAS MUCH BIGGER in the early 1900s, Gause says. "Pull boat crews could go in and stay in the woods a week at a time. They lived in camps. Pull boats were a unique way of getting logs out. They're flatboats that carry a portable steam engine. They're fitted out with drums and cables and can pull up to three-quarters of a mile in a straight line."

Gausee also describes the "gunboat" that is made to haul timber that won't float to the mill. "It is like a pontoon," he says. "Logs were anchored underneath it to be towed to market. In the earlier days, gunboats were a sort of oblong box made out of wood. Later they were made out of metal. A cable with hooks would pick up the logs and pull them under the gunboat where they would be anchored. There could be a long string of gunboats that were owned by the saw mills. Two well-known mills were Adams Saw Mill and Hallet Lumber Company."

Both Gause and his wife, Georgia, smile remembering the social life that they used to enjoy in the Delta, especially the barge parties. "It was a different world in the 1930s and '40s, wasn't it, Georgia?" Gause asks as he turns to his wife for confirmation that perhaps the good old days were the best days of all.

Gause says he once saw six or seven bear cubs climb a tree. "The mother stood watching out for her cubs," he says. "Then she climbed about halfway up the tree and signaled for them to come down. Bears leave their mark on trees. They reach as high as they can and scrape their claws along the tree. We also saw alligators and turtles, moccasins and water snakes. Sometimes when you were out floating, you'd bump into a tree, and it would knock a snake down into the boat. It didn't bother you though. It would go to the far end of the boat and curl up. You'd just throw out snakes with a paddle."

West Nile sickness is a concern today, and people still worry about mosquitoes. "They were always a problem in the swamp." Gause says. "You'd be swatting them all the time. A lot of people got malaria and had to be treated with quinine. There weren't any outboard motors then. If a man out with a logging crew got sick, someone would have to paddle out and get him. He'd take medicine and most likely recover."

"Tell about your birth," Georgia prompts her husband. She says she met him at Orange Beach when she was teaching the fifth grade.

Tom Gause laughs. "Dr. Hodgson delivered me," he says. "He wrote my birth in an old ledger. It said 'December 27, 1924. Male child delivered to Mary Warren Gause. $10.00.' There weren't but three or four doctors in the area then. One was a dentist, and he turned a wheel to operate his drill. There wasn't any electricity. Doc's name was Douglas Bryant."

"There is so much to remember," Gause says. He points at a hunting horn that decorates the wall of his den. "That's a cow's horn. I'll never forget that sound, the deep, long, haunting bellow of it. Dogs used to know that sound like no other. Blow on the horn, and they'd come running."

GAUSE SAYS LEE SHANKS lived in the last old mill house of Bacon-McMillan. "He got burned though, and he's not living there now, planting his plastic flowers. It's too bad. You know, he believed that the Devil didn't like flowers, and he'd stick 7-Up and Coke bottles all over his trees. He'd attach plastic flowers. Made an Eden right there on the road a stone's throw and a bit from where the Stagecoach Cafe is today. Things are changing in the Delta. It's becoming a playground now," he says.

But memories live on and become part of a living, indeed breathing, landscape of what Thoreau called "this vast, savage, howling mother of ours, Nature, who speaks a "tawny grammar," a mother-wit derived from the beauty and wildness of the earth and all of its expressions, human and animal alike.

Georgia and Tom Gause; he holds a caulking mallet used on the old wooden boats in the Delta to push caulking between the planks.

IT'S GOOD TO RECALL the past again, and Tom Gause might be found doing that at the coffee club that meets regularly at the Stagecoach Cafe. Maybe he'd be there with Leslie Smith and W. E. Slaughter who was responsible for the delivery of logs to the Bacon-McMillan Mill, and if one were privy to the stories being told, they might hear horns blow just like yesteryear. "Five blows! There'd be a problem at the pull boat. One very long blow, ooooooooh ooooooooooh, saying 'I'm opening the throttle. It's High Ball time!'" The sound signals getting together and its resonance lives in stories that keep being told. Gause reminds us through his oral history that we are the Delta; we are the place we are from. ∽

LEE SHANKS

Becoming Part of the Delta Environment

LEE Shanks's house on the road into Stockton lies idle now, its front yard, once his re-creation of Eden, has gone to weed. He lived in one of the last old mill houses connected with the Bacon-McMillan Mill, a place where workers lived free if they worked for the mill. Shanks, an African-American who was born around 1918 and who worked for McMillan cutting plywood, turned his mill-house with its tin roof into a sanctuary.

"The Devil don't like flowers," he said, sitting outside on his steps one early fall afternoon in 2003 while his old yellow dog tried to find a cool spot under a nearby table to shield himself from the sun.

"I don't remember when I was born," Shanks said. "I come from Shelby County. Ain't got no birth certificate, but I can tell you it's been longer than fifty years. I come from a time we did plowing by hoe."

Shanks said he was married but never had children. He says he had a wife, but what he wants to talk about is not people; it's his garden, his Eden come to life with the plastic flowers he purchased from a dollar store and the bottles he'd collected—green 7-Up bottles, Sprite, and Coke bottles that grace the ends of innumerable trees.

"I got heaven on my mind," Shanks says. "I asked the Lord what to do. The Devil is into drinking, smoking, telling lies and dipping, but he won't come round where flowers is in bloom." And in that case, he'll stay a far piece away from Shank's abode, for every plant, every shrub, has a plastic flower attached. Indeed, Shanks has a story that testifies to his claim. "Hurricane Erin tore through here in 1955, and it yanked down a big oak tree. Now it coulda gone right there through my livin'room, but it took and fell right near that old tree." He points to an ancient chinaberry tree at the corner of his house and smiles. "I got heaven on my mind," he says again.

SHANKS NO LONGER lives in his house in Delta land. In his back yard, a huge tree lies moldering into humus. He no longer collects flowers and bottles, or plants okra and peas as his papa used to do, for he was injured in a fire and is no longer able to care for himself and for his garden. In time, the house will be gone and even the weeds will have disappeared, but Lee Shank's place and his words are part of the storied Delta that will live on long after he and his garden have ceased to be. The *Mobile Register*, in the Sunday edition, March 3, 2002, printed a story that featured the old settler. A picture of Shanks's house and the clipping from the *Register* hangs on the wall in Stockton's Stagecoach Cafe, a part of their archives. ◟

DAVIDA HASTIE

An Authority on Delta History and Lore

DAVIDA Hastie sits uneasy with modernity. With an eye to future conservation, her memories dredge Delta days from a time when the river reckoned a different life, a time when double-enders, similar to skiffs or pirogues pointed on both ends, plied the waters, a time of pull-boats or barge-mounted skidders that winched felled logs through the swamp. Whistle boys would signal one another: "Go ahead. Come back. Stop," as they relayed orders from the foremen of skidding crews to the engineers of the pull boat.

"Logs used to be huge," Hastie says, sitting in a wicker chair on the back porch of her house. "Logging was a way of life. Loggers would come in and deaden the trees and float them out when there was a 'freshet' or time of high water. Trees couldn't be floated out if there wasn't enough water. Timber was the main source of income."

"The river was a dangerous place when I grew up," Hastie adds. "We never swam in it. People used to drown in the swamp if they didn't know how to handle the river right, but thinking changes with time. My own children not only swam in the rivers around Stockton, they would waterski up and down them."

An environmentalist, historian, and poet, Hastie likes to reminisce about the Delta. She says that people would come over from Mobile on weekends to enjoy barge parties, but the river afforded more than recreation. It marked the economy and tallied the timber trade. "When you're my age," she adds, "you go back to what happened in your childhood."

Storytelling is a way history escapes the past, and Davida Hastie balances the past and the present with equal ease, relating the Delta's history with the agility of someone who could "ride a log out" and cruise the swamp. The town of Stockton where she grew up and subsequently brought up her children was founded in 1834. It was incorporated in 1839, when William Kitchen sold his half interest in the town for $24,500 and became half owner of a stagecoach line.

"There weren't any deer, then," Hastie says, "and people did a lot of fox and squirrel hunting. The woods were full of otter, and possum. You can't get rid of possum and coon." She once had a pet coon that would ride up on the back seat of the car. "He loved to chew gum. He would take a piece of gum, chew it awhile, remove it with his paws, roll it around and around, put it back in his mouth and chew it some more. He wouldn't swallow it either. I guess he wondered why that gum never did chew up." Hastie explains that her pet was a dark coon. "He slept on top of the house up under the eaves, and he would come down when I called him: "Coonie, Coonie, Coonie."

HASTIE DIDN'T GO IN for fancy pet names—just called her animals cat, puppy, dog—or coon. "Coon" used to play with her little white Spitz, and the two animals, one dark and one light, would pummel each other. "Coonie had never tasted blood, but one day I shot a bird and gave it to him. After that he raided chicken yards, and I had to take him back to the wild."

Hastie's voice, full and throaty, speaks of William Bartram and the time he spent with Major Robert Farmer, Commandant of British West Florida, who lived within sight of the town of Stockton when it was located at the river. It was August 1778, when Bartram, in a trading boat, landed at Tensaw bluff. He wrote about the beautiful evergreen shrub, *myrica inodora*, about the wax tree that rises erect for nine or ten feet before it divides into a multitude of branches. Hastie says that she knows a few places where the *oenothera grandiflora* or large-flowered evening primrose with its rich golden blooms can still be found. She was instrumental in helping to establish the sixteen-mile Bartram Trail water route, so it is fitting that the trail marker is in Davida Hastie's front yard.

HASTIE SAYS THAT IN THE 1830S, the four-horse stage coach stopped in Stockton at Patrick Byrne's Tavern near Blakeley when making its 192-mile route to Montgomery. Mrs. Bryant had a tavern at Montgomery Hill. Travelers could buy breakfast for fifty cents and get a hearty supper of chicken pie, ham, five veggies, pudding and sauce and sweet pies, not to mention wine and brandy for only twenty-five cents more.

Hastie speaks somberly of Fort Mims, where the largest massacre in the United States during frontier times occurred up the road from her home. She wrote a poem about the Massacre and about Red Eagle, the mixed-race Indian leader. Two poignant stanzas confront the issue of William Weatherford's guilt because the blood of two races flowed in his veins. Hastie writes:

> Was he to fight his paleface brother
> Or support his mother's kin?
> Both bloods ran through his veins;
> Either way would seem a sin.
>
> . . . .

He'd ne'er forget that hot August noon
At Fort Mims; the curdling cry
Of friend and kin t'would haunt him
Until the day he'd die.

Red Eagle's mother was Sehoy III, a princess of the Wind Clan of Creek Indians. Her bones rest beside those of her son, keeping forever their uncertain peace. Davida Hastie's daughter, Lynn Hastie, is the author of *William Weatherford: His Country and His People.* The above stanzas were published in that definitive work.

Davida Hastie is herself legend, for she is often called the foremost authority on the Delta's folkways and history. For thirty-four years, from 1948 to 1982, she and her husband owned and ran Live Oak Lodge and Mobile Home Park. "It was way before the Interstate was built," she says. "There was just a dirt road, no electricity, and no running water. People would come to get boats, and we'd sell vienna sausage and bread and pork-and-beans." She said that folks would cook up squirrel along the river banks—flour it and fry it like chicken.

"There were three country doctors in the community in 1902 or 1903. Now there aren't any," Hastie says, but she keeps the environment on course for a productive future. One of her many contributions is getting a twenty-four-mile stretch of the thirty-five-mile Tensaw River reclassified as an Outstanding Alabama Water, the highest status of protection granted to a body of water in the state of Alabama. This classification keeps the river free of industrial discharge and damaging development. Although numerous newspaper articles attest to Davida Hastie's influence in Alabama, particularly with matters that relate to environmental concerns, she is modest and unassuming. She is generous with her time and willing to engage in any discussion about the Mobile-Tensaw Delta. ⌒

This stretch along the Bartram Canoe Trail has changed little since Red Eagle and other Creek Indians paddled it in wooden canoes.

Robert Leslie Smith and Clem Parnell, with an old car and a prop gun they use in parades in the Delta.

CLEM PARNELL

Protecting the Delta through Enforcement

STATE of Alabama Conservation Enforcement Officer Clem Parnell knows the Mobile-Tensaw Delta, knows the creatures of the swamp—the turtles and deer. He has many tales to tell about them and about those who have dared to break a law. "Sometimes," he says "people think that deep in the swamp at night, no one will know if they steal an endangered turtle or shoot a deer."

They are wrong.

Clem Parnell will, if necessary, sit on a river bank all night long waiting to catch the person he's after, a person who has transgressed and broken a law. And whoever he's waiting for is probably unaware of what is going to happen. Parnell might be dressed in ragged clothes and appear to be a fisherman. Anyone bent on taking protected game had better watch out. Clem Parnell is not the man to meet up with, for he could be creeping up behind to say, suddenly: "You're under arrest."

"People go out hunting deer at night," Parnell says, and explains that if someone is in a boat or is using a spotlight to find a deer, it isn't the same as using a spotlight on land. On the river, spotlights serve as a means of navigation, so it's difficult to say if a wrong is being done until the deer's head is blown off.

As Parnell's story unfolds, tension builds, and the image of the river and the deer stand out as if they were projected on a screen. Parnell is a master storyteller, and as he talks, characters come alive and the tale moves inexorably toward its climax. Parnell tells of a time some years past when he watched a houseboat, eyeing the comings and goings of its occupants as they slept by day and ranged the waters by night.

"They would get on an auxiliary boat tied to the houseboat and ease into the darkened river. One guy worked the tiller. The other sat in front with a rifle across his knees, shining a light up and down the riverbank. They couldn't see me; they didn't know anyone was watching."

Parnell reports that eight-mile venture with cinematic exactness. He tells of riding an ATV deep into the swamp for five miles before he got out of his vehicle to walk a final mile so the transgressors would not hear him coming. Parnell says he watched the houseboat and the men as they left on their nightly expedition. Then he tells how he "disrobed" on the river bank and swam in darkness to the boat.

I DIDN'T EVEN THINK about the fact that there might be alligators in the water. I just swam out to the houseboat and climbed aboard. I emptied one of the coolers the men had on board. It was just sitting there waiting to be filled with deer meat. I grabbed the emptied cooler, swam back to shore with it, put my gear in, and swam back to the boat again. By this time, the guys had moved up the river where they couldn't see me, so I eased under one of the bunk beds and waited. Pretty soon, I could hear the motor, putt putt putt putt, putt putt, sounding against the silence of the night. Then voices came close as the men tied up to the houseboat."

Parnell describes the men. "I can tell you, one of those men was BIG. He must have been six feet three, and I bet he weighed 360 pounds. I knew I had to take out that guy first. I pushed him up against the wall before he saw me." Parnell's voice, low and certain, gathers momentum as it edges toward a moment of narrative surprise: "That guy was so shocked to see me, there was no fight or flight left in him."

"Handcuffing the guy was a challenge," Parnell continues. "The guy's hands were so large, his arms so thick, they wouldn't go behind his back so that I could snap handcuffs on him. He had to hold them in front, and even then, I just barely managed to get the cuffs around his wrists.

"These guys thought there was just the two of them alone on the river that night. Just them—and the moon and the stars—and the deer they were out to catch. And there I appeared with my clothes dry. It was as if I materialized out of the air or dropped from a helicopter. I keep hearing this story repeated, but it's changed through the years. Some folks say it happened in the dead of winter, in February. They say I swam a river of ice. I didn't though; the capture happened in September. Others have said there were alligators swimming with me in the water. I don't know if a gator was there or not. I didn't even think about them. I was focused on arresting these guys."

PARNELL EXPLAINS how he put the deer hunters in their own auxiliary boat, took them ashore, and then walked them through the swamp to his ATV. "It was four o'clock in the morning and still dark. The men sat in the back with their legs hanging down, and by the time we got to my vehicle, their legs were cut up from the briars. It was then about 7 o'clock. The men served some jail time, and they had to pay several thousand dollars in fines. They lost their boat, motor, and we confiscated their guns and even the spotlight."

Another story Parnell tells concerns red-bellied turtles. "They bring in big money on the black market," he explains as he takes a swallow or two of cold sweet tea at the Stagecoach on a hot late July afternoon. Ice clinks against the class, and the story is launched. "I worked covert details," he says. "Once I was employed by a man to catch rare turtles. This guy wanted to see to it that the red-bellied turtle became extinct. He said he thought local wild-life officers were dumb. Easily tricked. Well, he was wrong. My friend, who also does covert work, and I glued ourselves to this guy trafficking in turtles." Parnell moves into the gist of his story. He explains the plan. "The turtle-catcher thought of himself as 'The Reptile Professor,' but he wasn't as smart as he thought. He outwitted himself. Wanted to be the only person in existence who had red-bellied turtles stocked in private ponds. He thought the federal government would give him a grant, and he would be the one to restock the whole area with red-bellied turtles. In the beginning, his restocking program would release only male red-bellied turtles. Then, when there were no new turtles, the government would come in and pay him again to release more turtles. And this time, he would release both males and females." Parnell says that the entire covert operation took a couple of years. "Quite a while," he says, "but the so-called 'professor' was caught and jailed."

Parnell describes the particularities of the black-market alligator snapping turtle trade. "There is a big market overseas," he says. A hundred-pound alligator snapping turtle can bring in about $250. A rare 150-200 pound turtle can bring as much as $5,000 in Japan. The person who wants to buy a turtle will call someone in Japan and ask him for 'X' amount of money. The turtle will be delivered to a restaurant. It'll be put in a huge aquarium that is suspended from the ceiling where it will be on display. It'll become a major tourist attraction. Restaurants even compete to see who has the most impressive turtle show."

Game warden Clem Parnell checking hunter Joe Burroughs's gun to make sure it complies with Alabama hunting regulations.

"There is also a market for Southern black knobbled sawback turtles," Parnell says. "These little turtles are about as big as a fifty-cent piece, and when they're tiny, they're absolutely beautiful. They sell in a pet shop for as much as thirty or forty dollars. People are fascinated with turtles. When they get to be about six to eight inches, though, they get ugly."

Parnell has spent time tracking the red-bellied turtle, and he says that its prime nesting place is Gravine Island. "It's near the place where the Tensaw River forks. There is a beach about a quarter of a mile long, and 90 percent of the red-bellied turtles lay eggs there."

The turtles, however, aren't safe. "Fish crows eat the eggs. They'll see turtles leaving their nests, and they'll go dig up the eggs and eat them. The fire ants are a special menace, too. They came over on banana boats from South America, and now they've spread all over the state." Parnell explains that fire ants also eat the eggs of non-harmful snakes that lay eggs in the dirt. "They even eat eggs that birds lay in nests three or four feet off the ground. The ants migrate up the bush, find the eggs and begin their feast."

PARNELL BELIEVES THAT FIRE ANTS are a scourge to our environment. The fire ant's enemy is a tiny fly that measures no more than one-sixteenth of an inch. Relish creeps into Parnell's voice as he explains the intricate tactics of the phorid fly. "Its only reason for existence is to eat fire ants. The phorid fly scouts out the territory, finds an ant colony, and selects an ant. It lands on the ant and injects an egg into the ant's body at the base of its neck. The egg hatches into larvae and subsequently becomes a fly maggot that enters the ant's head and begins to eat it from the inside out. The ant's head falls off, and a new fly emerges only to find another ant and start the process all over again. One female phorid fly can carry as many as a hundred eggs ready for

attack. The phorid fly doesn't attack all ants, however. It doesn't attack carpenter ants or the native ant species, and it doesn't bother humans or plants. The fly just goes after fire ants, and they're deadly scared of this fly. They'll get so scared that they hide out inside their mound, and sometimes they'll starve to death. Mississippi State University and Auburn University have conducted research on the phorid fly. This information is being released to control fire ants in Alabama."

CONSERVATION OFFICER PARNELL's territory encompasses the entire Delta. He has worked at this job for twenty-four years. "It's the best job that's ever been made. A lot of changes have taken place in the Delta, namely habitat destruction. In the last twenty-five years, the hardwood forests have disappeared. There used to be numerous stands of Longleaf pines, but these have been replaced by Loblolly pines. The name 'Loblolly,' it is said, means 'mud puddle,' and it is associated with this particular pine because it grows well on wet sites. It's also known as an 'old field pine.'" The tree is easily recognized by its long needles that are between five and nine inches long. The bark is thick, dark brownish red. The tree has a rounded top or crown and grows easily and fast on various sites. Unfortunately, the Loblolly is not structurally sound for lumber. It is used for plywood and paper.

Parnell believes that few black bears still roam the Mobile-Tensaw Delta. He says the black bear population is congregated in north Mobile County. "Everybody was raised on Winnie the Pooh," Parnell says, "but let me dispel a myth. Bears don't love honey like people think. They've even been known to destroy it. Bears eat baby bees, and those babies are pure protein. They love it."

The Alabama Black Bear Alliance, co-sponsored by the Alabama Wildlife Federation and the Nature Conservancy of Alabama, is dedicated to preserving the bear habitat and they are researching reintroducing the Alabama black bear into the Mobile-Tensaw Delta territory. Parnell stresses the fact that the process is far from easy. The bear mother-to-be has to be delivered to the area where she will give birth at just the right time. Timing is critical. If the mother bear is brought to the Delta too soon, she will roam away and give birth elsewhere. If handled correctly, however, the mother bear will give birth to babies who will consider the Delta home. "Baby bears," Parnell says, "usually stay with their mother until they're two. After that, Mama may attempt to leave the area and go back where she came from. The babies, having been imprinted, will stay. By the time they're grown, they'll consider the Delta their home."

A platform for use by paddlers along the Bartram Canoe Trail, which is in Clem Parnell's jurisdiction.

STUDIES HAVE SHOWN that bears can roam as much as twenty miles in a day, but during hunting season when the woods are filled with human scent, Parnell says the bears will narrow their range to a quarter of a mile. "The bears want to get away from hunters, so they'll go to the thickest, deepest, most humanly inhospitable area they can find, especially those places where there are ti ti bushes." For those less acquainted with the terrain than he, it sounds as if Parnell is saying "tide eye," bushes, so he pauses in his disputation on bears and spells "ti ti," explaining that the ti ti is like a large gooseberry bush. "Around 70 percent of the bear population now live in north Mobile County, but do you know why the bear population doesn't increase?" he asks. "It is due to habitat loss. The bear has nowhere to go. Habitat is critical," he says. "If bear territory is reduced, an old bear hunting a mate in season will kill a young bear. The youngster," Parnell says, "has to get out to save his own life. The young male is competition."

Parnell says that twenty-five to fifty years ago, people would shoot bears for eating feral hogs. "Today," he says, "bears are victims of road-kill, especially on Salco Road, off Highway 43. They get shot by hunters and have been shot by bee keepers as well."

An article by Sam Hodges in the *Mobile Register,* Sunday April 21, 2002, argues that "unless something is done to preserve their shrinking habitat, south Alabama black bears may face extinction." If they go, he says, "the state's entire bear population could follow."

A few bear facts mentioned by the *Mobile Register* include: The black bear is classified *Ursa americanus.* It is divided into subspecies, but the differences among the bears are minor. Black bears range over most of the United States, but they are no longer in many of the states where they originally roamed. Black bears vary in their degree of blackness. Some are brownish-black. Most have a tan muzzle. The size of black bears varies, but the typical bear is somewhere around five feet in height. Males weigh up to eight hundred pounds, but the average weight is closer to three hundred pounds. Females weigh, on average, two hundred pounds. Black bears have a keen sense of smell and hearing, and they can run thirty miles an hour. Despite their weight, bears are able to climb trees, and they are also good swimmers. Mating season occurs in the late spring and summer. Newborn baby bears weigh a pound or less and stay with their mothers for about a year and a half. In the Mobile-Tensaw Delta, black bears don't tromp about in drifts of snow, and they don't hibernate. They bed down on the ground in a nest of vegetation. Females are said to roam some eleven miles, but male bears, except during breeding season, range over sixty-six square miles.

Parnell's store of information regarding life in the Delta includes a few words about alligators. "Alligators are cold-blooded like lizards," Parnell adds, "but for a short distance, one can outrun a horse. It exhausts its supply of energy quite rapidly." He comments on the fact that the alligator doesn't chew its food, which plays into how they are caught. He explains that alligator poles have a dull metal hook attached to a line. The alligator will swallow the hook. This will enable it to be pulled out of the water. The line is cut, and the alligator can then be moved to a safer area where it can more easily be dealt with. And then, the digestive juices in its stomach can dissolve wood or metal, so the hook does it no permanent harm.

It seems as if everyone in and around Stockton knows Clem Parnell. In the Stagecoach Cafe, people ease up to where he is sitting and start talking. The officer's phone rings and rings. He holds it up and comments: "I can't get away from this thing." The Delta, doubtless, is his priority. It claims his nights as well as his days, and even when he is supposed to be off-duty, he is called for an investigation or to go to court. "We are mandated to work only forty hours per week," Parnell explains, "so we have to use our time wisely to maintain this."

Listening to Clem Parnell talk about his job and about the Delta is like participating in a grand adventure. He is a compendium of information about the environment and the Mobile-Tensaw Delta and its habitants. He knows the comings and goings and the activities of turtles, spiders, alligators, bears, and of human kind, poachers involved in assorted illegal transgressions. ◡

Opposite: *A wary alligator guarding its nest.*

FLOYD E. WOOLEY

Giving Room to the Delta's Creatures

YOU couldn't see the sun for the ducks," Floyd Wooley says, his eyes alight with the joy of remembering the Delta of the '50s and his boyhood. "When I was fourteen or fifteen," he says, "I used to take Senator Frank Boykin fishing. He carried this big wad of bills secured with a rubber band, and usually gave me $10.00. One day Mr. Boykin dropped his stash of money in the water and was fishing around with his hands trying to reach it. 'Pete's swimming around,' I said.

"'Pete?' he asked, looking around and not seeing a soul in the water.

"'He's gonna get your money or bite your hand off,' I said. I didn't tell him who Pete was. Thought he'd figure it out directly. That money was just bobbin' along on top of the bay. Mr. Boykin grabbed an oar, reached over the side of the boat, fished it out, and dried it off."

"I'll never forget Mr. Boykin," Wooley says. "During duck season, he'd wear a Shriners' hat with a red tassel. He'd wave it in the air, and shout 'Damn the torpedoes. Full speed ahead.' I'd laugh, and he'd say it again. 'Full speed ahead,' and we'd be on our way seeing how many fish we'd catch this particular outing."

Floyd Wooley makes it clear that one alligator is simply not like another, and this is where Pete comes in. Wooley says he could tell Pete from any other gator just by the shape of his mouth. Pete made his home in water behind the Silver King Restaurant on the Causeway, and he was Wooley's prize pet. "I

used to feed him by hand," Wooley says. "At first I'd put brown mullet or large croakers on a fishing pole, and he'd swim right up and snatch them. Then it got to where I could feed Pete right out of my hand." If Pete had been a puppy with floppy ears and fetching eyes, Wooley couldn't have spoken of him with more affection. "Once when the tide had dropped down and I was feeding Pete," Wooley recounts, "I slipped on the steps and fell in with him. I just put my hand on Pete's head and pushed myself back on the bank. He never moved, that gator, but his head was like a rock. Turned out Pete was a girl, though," Wooley says, laughing. "He had children."

IT IS NOT HARD TO IMAGINE that most people didn't feel about Pete as Floyd Wooley did, certainly not a woman who was out crabbing one day. "She was sitting on the bank, baiting her line with chicken bones, and planning on supper, "Wooley explained. "All of a sudden she was pulling in her line, running it right between her legs, when she realized it wasn't a crab she'd hooked. It was Pete. That woman yelled so loud she could be heard in Pensacola. She rolled backward off that log like she was turning somersaults." Wooley said that Pete didn't just swim away and disappear. "He hung around the Oyster House until somebody shot him." Wooley tried to get another alligator, but he said "there wasn't another like Pete."

"The Delta is not like it used to be," Floyd Wooley says, his voice soft with remembering. "I used to ride all over Chocolatta

Bay when I was a boy of nine or ten. My dad and I used to catch shrimp for the Silver King Restaurant. Back then the State would put you in jail if you caught shrimp under sixty-count. There were a lot of shrimp in the bay back then, especially over by the tunnel."

Wooley remembers catching a seventy-two-pound catfish. He was twelve years old and fishing by himself. "I was trying to haul in this big cat, but he was twisted around my line. I stuck my hand in the fish's mouth, and he clamped down hard. Those pads in his mouth felt like sandpaper. I grabbed him around the jaw and pulled him in the boat. Later we skinned him and cut him into steaks."

WOOLEY SPEAKS of his high school buddies, Sonny Rayford and Buddy Botter, who used to spend summers exploring Chocolatta Bay. They'd tie up their boat, cut cane and sing, "Gimme land, lots of land. Don't fence me in." One day, just as the boys were about to sit down on a log, it moved. Wooley says that "the thing that seemed a log was two huge cottonmouth moccasins with their mouths wide open."

Wooley knows the creatures of the Delta, and he gives them room. "I'm afraid of muskrats," he says. "They've got big teeth." He tells about how trappers put up poles and stretched the skins. "They'd dry them and sell them for furs," he explained. "The nutria have nearly killed out the muskrats." Wooley explained how the nutria [a large rodent] tunnels under marsh grass, eats its roots, and kills it from underneath. Hundreds of acres of marsh grass are being lost in the Delta.

He says that "people today like to blame the problems in the Delta on the people living there, but it is more complicated than that. There isn't enough rain." Wooley believes that dams have cut the water flow. "There used to be swift currents, but the flow isn't there now," he says. "And there used to be fifteen to twenty feet of water back behind the Oyster House. Now, there is only a couple of feet of water. Things aren't like they used to be. Not like they used to be," he says.

GLENN SEBASTIAN

Mapping the Territory of the Rivers

To speak with Glenn Sebastian, Chair of the Department of Geography at the University of South Alabama, is to experience the world anew. Dr. Sebastian clearly enjoys talking about the Mobile-Tensaw Delta, and it is easy to be caught up in his enthusiasm. His fingers move, illustrating a tributary, a stream, a meandering river. His words map the territory scripted by the rivers.

Dr. Sebastian says that the most important changes that have affected the area of Mobile, the Delta, and the Bay (he speaks of them as one, as a unity) relate to sea level changes, to the erosion and the deposition brought about by the melting of glaciers that once covered most of northern America numerous times during the Plio-Pleistocene epoch. "There were major climatic changes," Sebastian says. "The earth, on average, was about seven degrees colder than it is today.

The Delta is the drainage of millions of years. During the glacial periods, more and more snow fell, and then it began to melt. The glaciers began to move southward, and the discharge of rivers created complex deltaic landforms like the Mobile-Tensaw Delta.

"Ten thousand years aren't anything to a geographer," he adds. "Did you know that ten thousand years ago, humans lived in north Alabama in Russell Cave?"

There are different types of deltas, and Sebastian names and accounts for them, beginning with the Arculate or fan-shaped delta, of which the Nile is an example. It is a wave-dominated delta that occurs when there is high wave energy. Outflow acts as a counter-current that slows the oncoming wave crests so that they break in deeper than usual water. The refraction of freshwater plumes creates a mix of sediments so that the deposited material forms a beach or sand bar at the shoreline. It is deltoid in shape.

The Mississippi Delta is referred to as a "bird-foot delta," Sebastian says. It has a shelf that deepens abruptly and thus creates thin extensions that carry sediment away in a pattern that forms a kind of bird's foot. Another delta that is defined by its name is the Cuspate or tooth-shaped delta. Sediment is pushed on both sides of the river mouth so that makes it look like the coastline is growing a tooth. "The Tiber River of Italy is a Cuspate delta," Sebastian says, drawing a toothy cusp on a handy piece of paper to illustrate his point.

"Our delta," Sebastian says, "is an estuarine delta." The Mobile, Tensaw, Apalachee, and Blakeley rivers flow into Mobile Bay and the Gulf of Mexico where the fresh water and salt water meet. "The amount of sediment," Sebastian explains, "depends on the volume of water flow, on how big that flow is and on how fast it is moving."

In addition to being a geographer, Glenn Sebastian is a story teller, and it is pleasant to imagine spending time on his boat, riding the river, and docking on Gaillard Island which, he says, was "once called "Doughnut Island." A Mobile dentist

named Wilson Gaillard, the founding father of the Mobile Bay Audubon Society, suggested making an island so there would be some place to deposit the dredge that was blocking the Bay. "Wilson thought the birds might like it," Sebastian says. Now the place has become a bird sanctuary, a thirteen hundred-acre triangular island habitat for brown pelicans, ospreys, gulls, herons, egrets, black skimmers, and terns.

Another fascinating story that Sebastian tells, one illustrated with sound effects, is that of the Mothball Fleet. "Have you ever been to Hurricane?" he asks, easing into a tale about World War II boats that were docked at Hurricane, a tiny town on the edge of the Delta, up along the river, off Highway 59. "Huge boats were lined up five across and then another five across, and another five, and another." As boats went up the river, the ghost ships would touch each other, and the boom boom boom, ta boom, ta boom issued its ghostly sound.

After World War II, a canal was dredged from the Tensaw to the Mobile River to accommodate Liberty ships sent there for storage and perhaps for future use. Hundreds of ships were stored in the Tensaw and other rivers. Eventually, the ships were either sold or taken out into the Gulf and sunk to make artificial reefs. "I used to go to Hurricane thirty-five years ago," Sebastian says, but "it's been a long time. A long time. Well, not so long, if geological time is the measure."

STORIES, MORE LASTING than the effects of glacial melt, are not bound by months and hours and days, or even epochs and ages. They are timeless, and Glenn Sebastian's Delta tales will be around as long as there is someone to read them, talk about them, and remember.

"All evidence points toward a rise in sea level over the past fifteen thousand years when the shore was anywhere from 66 to 148 meters below present sea level," Sebastian explains. "This would place it over one hundred kilometers seaward of the present mouth of the Bay. Mobile Bay would have been a deep river valley," he says, illustrating height, depth, and width with his arms. It seems as if he is magically constructing the Delta with his hands, creating its majesty and mystery, the rise and fall of his voice expressing the river's fluctuation and flow. "As the sea advanced into the ancestral Mobile River valley," he says, "it became an estuary and the valley began to fill with sediment. Even today, this process continues. Goes on and on," he says, his voice trailing off to indicate the unfolding of it.

Sebastian believes that two of the more significant geological changes are the drowning and filling of not only the ancestral channel of the Mobile River itself, but also the tributaries that entered the river in the area now covered by the Bay and the shoreline deposits that formed the Fort Morgan Peninsula and Dauphin Island. The formation of the Delta occurred in the last five thousand years as the infilling of the bay occurred. If the progradation of the Delta continues at the rate of twenty centimeters per century, the Bay will be filled with alluvial sediment in less than fifteen hundred years.

The earth is constantly undergoing change, and Glenn Sebastian gets out a pad and pencil to explain some of the marvels associated with it. He explains the nature of faults, showing how slippage or displacement along the plane creates a breakage in the earth. "Faults are often of great horizontal extent," he says. "A fault line can run along the ground for several miles." He mentions the Mount Vernon fault and defines graben and horst. "A graben is a ditch or depression. A horst is an uplift," he says, as he presses his hands together to show how pressure results in slippage.

Dr. Glenn Sebastian is revered on the University of South Alabama campus by students and colleagues alike. Those who have graduated look back on their university days and single him out as a master teacher they'll never forget. They especially remember the field trips he leads to such interesting places as Big Bend National Park, the Gulf Islands National Seashore, and Mammoth Cave National Park. It may be said, as well, that his tastes are deliciously eclectic. The professor might be found not only on a boat on Chacaloochee Bay, but sitting at a local restaurant talking about seafood and eating oysters with a group of Odyssey students he has volunteered to instruct in the culinary arts. Anyone would be fortunate, indeed, to pull a chair up to his table. ↩

Opposite: *A red-headed woodpecker.*

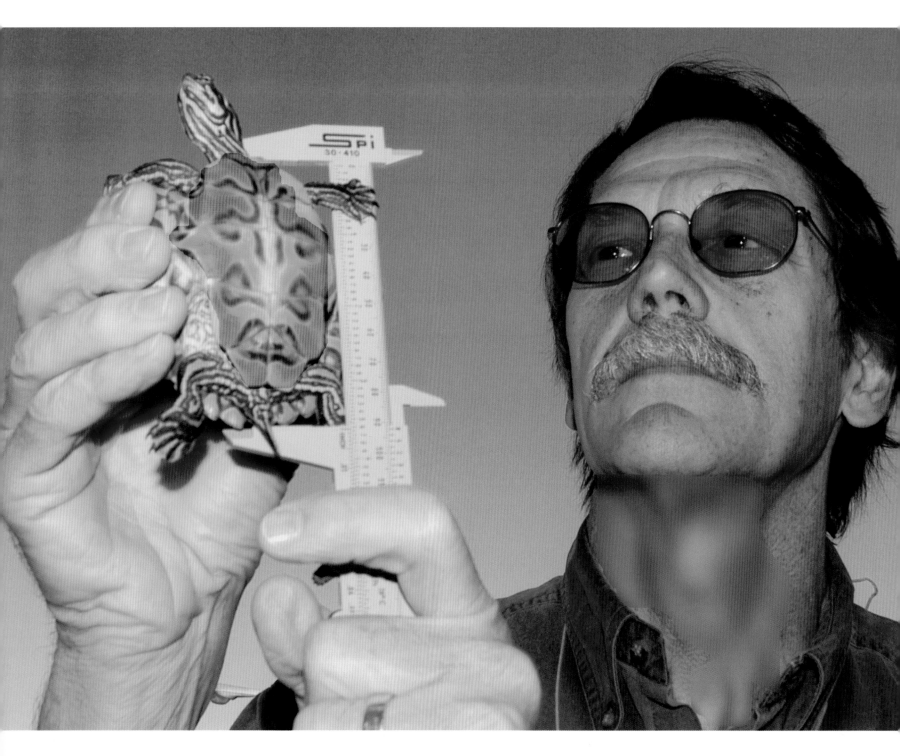

David Nelson

Using the Swamp as a Classroom

A biology professor at the University of South Alabama, David Nelson defines himself as a vertebrate ecologist and stresses the fact that plants and animals are interdependent. Everything has its place. Plants and animals beautify, embellish, and make habitable the earth that humans share and enjoy. "Part of our existence is tied up with nature," Nelson says, and his voice registers the intensity of his conviction that "nature restores the soul." He speaks of its wonder and its mystery and states how exciting and intriguing it is to experience firsthand a place like the Mobile-Tensaw Delta.

"We do our children a disservice if we teach them to fear nature. In 'the swamp,' there are wonders that people seldom see anywhere else are everywhere."

He cites the beauty of the mud snake that has a red-iris eye. Speaking of it with respect, as if of a friend, he mentions the snake's docility and tells how it feeds on salamanders. He comments on the glossy crawfish snake and of the red, yellow, and black coloring of the rainbow snake. The latter, he says, grows to be five feet long, maybe longer, and it comes out at night. "They are rare and non-poisonous," Nelson says, "but we don't know a whole lot about them." He points out that snakes keep growing as long as they are alive.

Nelson spends time in the swamp as well as in the classroom, and he is an authority on snakes. "The king snake, corn and rat snake are mammal eaters and they afford a kind of natural control and balance in the often elusive and mysterious life that goes on in the swamp," he says. "It is too bad if fear affects how a person reacts."

"There are some fifteen to eighteen species of snakes in the Mobile-Tensaw Delta," Nelson says. The poisonous snakes include the Diamondback rattlesnake, the pygmy rattlesnake, the cottonmouth, and the coral snake that is the most venomous. It is small, though, and can't really get its fangs into something as large as a human unless they put their hands in the wrong place. Nelson's students are told to watch where they put their hands and their feet. They are taught to watch out for snakes, but Nelson says that snakes will get away from humans if they can. "Snakes have gotten bad press, but they serve a useful purpose in controlling rodents that can have some fifteen to twenty babies every thirty days or so."

B IOLOGY WAS NOT Nelson's initial choice of a career. As a student at Baylor University, he was enrolled in pre-med. "Then I discovered ecology when I was a senior. I decided to go into biology." He subsequently received his M.A. degree at Baylor and his Ph.D. at Michigan State.

Continuing a discussion of nature and specifically the Mobile-Tensaw Delta, Nelson says that wildlife will escape whenever possible. One of his more interesting encounters in "the swamp" occurred the second year he was at the University of

Opposite: *Taking field measurements of a red-bellied turtle.*

South Alabama. He had set out food traps and discovered that his net was holding a six-foot alligator gar. "I wanted to undo its teeth so it could escape, but they were about one-and-a-half inches long. I didn't want to be the gar's feast for the day, but I managed to free it from the net. It swam away."

Nelson is an authority on Alabama's endangered red-bellied turtle, the official state reptile. He has studied its distribution and has conducted telemetry studies to determine that the turtle's range is seven miles north and south. He has flushed the stomachs of the turtles to learn what they feed upon, and he has studied their nesting patterns to determine how many eggs they lay. The red-bellied turtle occurs most often in the confined area between the Causeway and I-65.

Snakes, alligators, and red-bellied turtles aren't the only valued habitants of the Delta's wild. There is the gulf sturgeon that must be protected and the bald eagle which Nelson says is seen less and less in the Delta. The osprey nests in the Delta, but it is not on the endangered list. Even mosquitoes have their place, and Nelson says that in spite of the fact that they are pests and he has to put on repellant to protect himself, he would defend their right to exist, along with spiders, roaches, and ants.

David Nelson is at home in nature, in the murky swamp and woodlands, but he is also at home in the classroom. Students seek him out to show him what they find. They know he will give them attention, and even during an interview, one student doesn't hesitate to come in with a plastic container holding a snake he has found on the road. The student pulls out a cottonmouth and shows it with pride, placing his fingers just at the right spot to cause the snake to open its mouth and display its fangs. Nearby a person with an impressive fear of snakes gets up gingerly, backs up, and eyes the snake cautiously. "Touch it," the student says as if the snake is a presentation, a gift of the wild and a ready lesson to be savored. The ophidiophobic reaches out two fingers of her hand and tentatively rubs them along the back of the snake. Nelson smiles as if to say "See, this is part of the wonder—the fact that the cottonmouth isn't scaly. It's ridged but smooth." He seems to know that the snake-fearing person would be changed by the experience and go forth to tell the story, tell about nature, its awesome wonder, even participate in the balanced and reciprocal exchange of life in which there is an acceptance of all that nature offers.

He believes—and teaches— the value of nature. Every one should be a responsible steward of nature and specifically of the Delta. Nature can cope with such things as periodic flooding, even hurricanes, but it is a disaster if we don't look after and preserve the wilderness at hand. The Mobile-Tensaw Delta is a place where people can go to be renewed, where they can leave city life behind, enter into the wilderness—body and soul—enter a spiritual world of beauty, mystery, and wonder and be transformed. ❧

Opposite: *Frogs and other amphibians are barometers of the Delta's health.*

GREGORY A. WASELKOV

Finding the Secrets of the Moundbuilders

As a professor of anthropology and director of the Center for Archaeological Studies at the University of South Alabama, Greg Waselkov put Bottle Creek on the map. Prior to his map-work begun in 1990, Andrew Bigelow's sketch map of 1853 provided the only detailed view of the area. Bigelow originally identified nine mounds. Waselkov's preliminary map featured fifteen mounds. Later fieldwork led to the discovery of Mounds P through R. The site today is known to consist of eighteen earthen mounds that date from A.D. 1250–1550.

To reach the Bottle Creek site, it is necessary to walk through wild forest. The dense palmettos and the extensive undergrowth absorb sound, so Waselkov warns that it is easy to get lost. The area is secluded. It requires a climb up a sandy bank and a quarter-mile or more walk through muck in moccasin territory before reaching it. The swamp is no place for the squeamish.

The Indians of Bottle Creek were water-oriented, and they traveled largely by canoe. Because the area floods every year, Waselkov explains that the Indians who lived on the mounds would have had to leave during times of flooding. "Only the two tallest mounds," he says, "would have been free of water."

One of Waselkov's favorite Bottle Creek artifacts is a small effigy of a human head. It is perfect in appearance and bears the comb of hair on top of the head. He explains that infants' heads were placed on cradleboards in order to achieve the desired pointed dimension at the back. Child-rearing in the Mobilian culture was matrilineal. The child was considered part of the mother's family. Often uncles were the ones who handled the discipline. "They did not depend so much on authority figures as consensus in governing," Waselkov says. Their council would have been one of elders.

Before coming to the University of South Alabama in 1988, Waselkov taught at Auburn and specialized in the Creek Indian culture. Speaking of their medical practices, he says the Mobilians treated illness by purifying the body and ridding it of any spirits that were causing harm. Thus it was customary to drink a quart or more of black tea that would cause them to throw up. They also effected steam baths that would induce sweating. The shaman, then, would warn against offending animal spirits.

Waselkov says that one interesting aspect in regard to Bottle Creek subsistence was the maize agricultural activity, and he has been obtaining soil test samples that produce paleoethonobotanical evidence. "A lot of research still needs to be done at Bottle Creek," Waselkov says. Fortunately, since 1915 state law has offered special protection to archaeological mound sites. It is a crime to remove archaeological materials without proper authorization.

Bottle Creek represents only one aspect of Gregory Waselkov's work. His book, *Old Mobile Archaeology*, preserves the past, moves it into the present, and opens to view that which is still to be learned. ↬

Waselkov examines an artifact from an Indian excavation site.

KAY FRIEDLANDER

Promoting Stewardship of the Delta

KAY Friedlander was the inspiration behind this book on the Mobile-Tensaw Delta, the driving force that made it happen because of her dedication to environmental issues and concerns. "The Delta needs a book devoted to it, to preserve its beauty and majesty," she says.

Friedlander moved to Fairhope in 1996 and became involved with Mobile's National Estuary Program. "I began to educate myself about Mobile Bay and its problems, about pollution, and about our natural and cultural history," she says. "The Delta is a cleansing force. We need to take a vested interest in it and the quality of life in the area in which we live."

In her work on the board of directors of the Alabama Coastal Foundation, an organization whose mission is to improve the quality of Alabama's coastal resources through education, cooperation, and participation, Friedlander actively promotes responsible stewardship. She would like to see more people join environmental organizations. "We are all spiritually affected by the environment," she says. "Human culture functions in a reciprocal relation with nature and creates a sense of wholeness that helps us put our lives into perspective."

The link between arts and sciences is important to Friedlander, and in her mind, the two form a unity. We need not adhere to boundaries created by disciplines. Rather we should engage in an exchange of ideas, a "unity of culture" such as that espoused by Murray Gell-Man, winner of the 1969 Nobel Prize in physics when he said in an interview with Bill Moyers that although it is important to learn a discipline thoroughly, it does not mean that knowledge should not be shared between history and literature, law and biology, and philosophy and any other field of knowledge that helps us understand and preserve the environment. This is especially applicable to the Mobile-Tensaw Delta.

The Master Environmental Education Program is one of the ways that Friedlander says people can be educated about the Delta and about the ecology. This program is run through the Baldwin County Extension Office of Auburn University. It offers an eight-and-a-half week training course in which mentors go into schools to teach about such things as the water cycle and about household hazardous waste.

"Educational awareness," she says, "is the key to the future." ∽

EDWARD O. WILSON

Scientist in His Own Back Yard

EDWARD O. Wilson says that the Delta is more than a natural reserve; it is a poetic place, a site of mystery and a spiritual resource as well. "There are few places in the world," he says "where you can leave the city and head into a wilderness in less than an hour."

A native son, an Alabamian who lived on Charleston Street in downtown Mobile in 1941-1942, a world renowned entomologist and biological theorist as well as the winner of two Pulitzer prizes, Edward Wilson has within him something of the enthusiastic thirteen-year-old teen who rode his bicycle over the causeway from Mobile to Spanish Fort reveling in the wetlands environment. The soft susurration of the South lingers in his voice as Wilson grants an early morning interview. He is "home" for a graduation commencement address at the University of South Alabama where he will also receive an honorary doctorate. While eating a breakfast of grits and crab quiche, he talks about the Mobile-Tensaw Delta in the days of his youth. He tells of the formative years he spent in Mobile." I used to collect butterflies." he says, "and found the first colony of fire ants in 1942 in the vacant lot next to my house on Charleston Street. I dreamed of going to the tropics and being an explorer. I had the *National Geographic* virus."

Wilson speaks of his early decision to become an entomologist, long before he used that word to describe his impressive career. "I wanted to go far from home and penetrate unknown places," Wilson says. "Let me put it this way. The Amazon, to me, is the Delta writ large. It is a miniature wilderness, exotic, mysterious, and had the reputation of being impenetrable. I wanted to penetrate the unknown places."

It would seem, almost, as if fifty-one years had vanished as quickly as the black bear Wilson chased when he was a senior at Harvard University, conducting a study of fire ants back home in Mobile. Driving along the highway, he says he saw a small black bear heading toward nearby woods. "Stop the car," he shouted to the driver. "I dashed out of the car and sprinted toward the bear. It was struggling to get through a fence. I was almost up to it," Wilson says, "when it squirmed through. "What did I think I was going to do?' he asks. "Well, that's part of the mystery."

Wilson describes himself as a Southern writer converted to scientist. He says that writers such as Barry Lopez, Bill McGibben, and Peter Matthiessen were poets first, and then they became naturalists. He thinks that the Delta needs to be preserved in language, in poetry. "We need a Mobilian Thoreau to write on the Delta," he says.

In the Prologue to *The Future of Life*, Wilson writes an intriguing letter to Henry David Thoreau, telling him that "at Walden Pond, the lamentation of the mourning dove and the green frog's *t-r-r-oonk!* across the predawn water were the true reason for saving this place." In the deep South, the Mobile-Tensaw Delta must be saved, too—the red bellied turtle, the black bear, the bald eagle and alligator. Except for care, they will become extinct.

Wilson says that the Delta has authenticity and a quality of indigenousness. The grand sweep of biological diversity is present in the plants and animals of 'the swamp," in the green-fly orchid, the tiny-leaved buckthorn, the rare sarvis holly, seventeen species of turtles, forty species of snakes, ten species of lizards, and twenty of frogs. To Wilson, Mobile and the Delta are the slice of home that he preserves in his soft, still southern voice and in his work, especially in *Naturalist,* the book that talks about growing up in around Mobile and exploring the Delta.

Wilson says there ought to be a stewardship of nature that is "based on the best understanding of ourselves and the world around us that science and technology can provide. . . . We will be wise to listen carefully to the heart, then act with rational intention and all the tools we can gather and bring to bear." The scientist takes another taste of grits and smiles. He is glad to be "home" and vows to return again—soon. ✑

Beavers are the Delta's engineers.

IN THE REALM OF RIVERS

View along Chacoloochee "Whiskey Ditch."

IN THE REALM OF RIVERS

An inquisitive raccoon, the "swamp bandit."

Almost hidden alligator.

In the Realm of Rivers

Alligator with golden clubs in sunlight.

Closeup of an osprey.

Opposite, top: *Alligator near its nest;* bottom: *mother alligator with its young on its head.*

Old-growth cypress.

IN THE REALM OF RIVERS

IV.

Then and Now

THE Mobile-Tensaw Delta is culturally, historically, and environmentally diverse. Indian Mounds still register the lives of Native Americans. The Delta is marked by war, that of the Fort Mims Massacre and the Siege of Blakeley, the tragic last major battle of the Civil War, fought after the war was officially over because the news of Lee's surrender had not yet reached the ears of the local commanders.

The dates that figure in the Delta's history are fluid and the years and months and days are sometimes reported differently. Nevertheless, the chronology speaks to a way of life that is preserved through stories handed down over the passing years. L. J. Newcomb Comings and Martha M. Albers's *A Brief History of Baldwin County* and Kay Nuzum's *A History of Baldwin County*, Shirley Bolton's *Baldwin County Sheriff's History, 1829-1994*, Charles Rodning's fine article, "El Río e Bahia del Espíritu Santo: Sense of Place," published in *Literary Mobile*, Leslie Smith's as yet unpublished "Gone to the Swamp," and Lynn Hastie's *William Weatherford: His Country and His People* all address the way the Delta is viewed, then and now.

Leslie Smith of Stockton says that "in the 150-year period ending roughly with World War II, most residents of north Baldwin County drew much of their sustenance from "the Swamp." He writes:

> Timber, farm products, fish, animal skins, meat and Spanish moss were gleaned from it and sold commercially. Hogs, cattle and horses were transported to its depths for grazing after the spring floods and removed at the first sign of high water, which was the name given to the periodic flooding. From European man's first appearance in this country until the day of the railroad, roughly Civil War time, he used the deeper water of the swamp for transporting himself and his possessions to and from the nearest point to his chosen home site on high ground. The home site

of choice was as close to the swamp as he could get and still be on high ground near a father spring of flowing water. As these sites were taken he had to content himself with a site farther away where a well could be dug.

This wooded territory was both Swamp and the Piney Woods that were located on higher ground. The ground afforded relief from the illnesses of the swamp which were malaria and yellow fever. It was not known then that "the fever" was caused by the mosquito, but it was determined that folks in the swamp got sick in the hot sticky summers when insects were about.

Perhaps a brief chronology can best present what happened in and around the Mobile-Tensaw Delta and lend perspective to some of the changes that have occurred throughout the years.

1540

The first battle between Indians and whites was fought in 1549 at Choctaw Bluff near Dixie Landing in north Baldwin County between DeSoto and his soldiers and the Choctaw Indians. Chief Tuscaloosa—for whom the river, the city, and the county were named and whose name means "Black Warrior"— surrendered to the Spanish as he was unable to stand further siege against his walled city of Mauvilla (this name has been variously spelled; the spelling used by the DeSoto Commission is Mabila). Dr. Herbert Hilary Holmes, in "Some Historical Facts About Tensaw," printed in *A Brief History of Baldwin County,* says that "a skeleton unearthed by [his] father and uncle on the banks of Pine Log Creek, together with the copper buttons and insignia on the casket, was identified as that of a soldier of DeSoto."

1721

Tensa (variously spelled Taensa, Taensas, and Tensaw, its current spelling) Indians lived on the bluff in the area that is now Stockton. This land later became the territory of the Creeks.

1778

William Bartram explores the Mobile-Tensaw Delta. In the account of his travels, Bartram writes that on August 5, he

set off from Mobile up the river in a trading boat, and was landed at Taensa bluff, the seat of Major Farmer, to make good my engagements, in consequence of an invitation from that worthy gentleman, to spend some days in his family; here I obtained the use of a light canoe to continue my voyage up the river. The settlement of Taensa is on the site of an ancient town of a tribe of Indians of that name, which is apparent from many artificial mounds of earth and other ruins. . . . In my excursions about this place, I observed many curious vegetable productions, particularly a species of Myrica (*Myrica inodora*): this very beautiful evergreen shrub, which the French inhabitants call the Wax tree, grows in wet sandy ground about the edges of swamps; it rises erect nine or ten feet, dividing itself into a multitude of nearly erect branches, which are garnished with many shining deep green entire leaves of a lanceolate figure; the branches' abundance of large round berries, nearly the size of bird cherries, are covered with a scale or coat of white wax; no part of this plant possesses any degree of fragrance. It is in high estimation with the inhabitants for the production of wax for candles, for which purpose it answers well with beeswax, or preferably, as it is harder and more lasting in burning.

1780

Lynn Hastie, in *William Weatherford: His Country and His People,* says that William Weatherford (Red Eagle) was born on April 28, 1780. Addressing the ancestry of Weatherford, the

A scene along the Bartram Canoe Trail is much the same as during Bartram's own journey.

author begins her book with the following scene:

William Weatherford sat on the bluff overlooking the dark flowing waters of the Alabama River. He could not remember a time when he had thought of himself as being anyone other than a Creek Indian, though in reality, he was a half-blood. Due to his mixed ancestry, he walked in two worlds—the red and white. Nevertheless, he had always been of one spirit. His mother was Sehoy, the third in succession of the princesses of the Wind Clan and the most interesting woman in the nation in her time. In the Muscogee tongue, her name meant "Two-Kept-On-After-The-Enemy." His father was Charles Weatherford, an Englishman who had come into the Creek Nation some years prior to 1778 from Georgia, in the company of Samuel Mims.

1784

Samuel Mims (1747–1813) moved to what was then Spanish West Florida and began acquiring land in the vicinity of Lake Taensas (as it was then spelled) near the confluence of the Alabama and Tombigbee rivers. In 1787, he obtained, by grant from the Spanish Governor at New Orleans, a large tract of land on Nanna Hubba Island. Here he built a home on the 524 acres that in 1813 became the site of Fort Mims.

Mims was among the more renowned settlers who lived in the Mobile-Tensaw Delta. The son of Benjamin Mims, he was born in Albemarle County, Virginia, in 1747. Mims was land-wealthy and owned considerable property in North Carolina, but nevertheless joined the American Revolution and served under Francis Marion, "the Swamp Fox." After the Revolution he gave his North Carolina lands to his brother, Thomas, and moved farther south to what was then the American frontier.

In 1788, Mims married Hannah Bready, who bore him three sons and three daughters: Joseph, David, Alexander, Harriett, Sarah, and Prudence.

1790

In the 1790s Stockton was a popular community in south Alabama. Some of the early families who lived in the area were the Aikens, Bryants, Bryars, Hasties, Kennedys, Kitchens, McMillians, Richardsons, Robinsons, Smiths, and Weeklys. Stockton was situated on the banks of the Tensaw River near what is known today as Bryant's Lower Landing. The landings afforded places for fisherman to launch their boats, for in addition to lumbering, the area was a fishing paradise. Hunting was also an indulgence, for the woods provided bountiful deer, squirrel, turkey, fox, and raccoon as well as quail and dove in the upland fields.

1799

John Pierce established the first school in Baldwin County and in Alabama. Referred to as the "Blab School" because studies were conducted orally in a number of languages such as English, French, Spanish, and Native American, the school was a one-room construction that was attended by lumbermen and "half-breeds." Red Eagle was one of the pupils who studied at the school along with the Mimses, Halls, Steadhams, Byrnes, McGillivrays, Taits, Durants, and McQueens. The school had no fixed terms, and John Pierce, who was also postmaster of the area, called school off when the farm season warranted. John Pierce died in 1827 at the age of seventy but left his mark on the Mobile-Tensaw area, especially on industry and education.

1802

John and William Pierce built a cotton gin on Boatyard Lake on the Alabama River.

1804

An itinerant Methodist preacher, Lorenzo Dow, en route from Mississippi to Georgia, stopped for six days in Tensaw. He held camp meetings and was said to have been the first Protestant minister in the area.

1805

The United States government granted the Creek Indians rights to establish a horse path for travel and to maintain it forever. This path evolved into the "Old Federal Road" that extended from the Ocmulgee River in Georgia to Fort Stoddard and St. Stephens.

Local travelers could go by way of Montgomery Hill, Old Fort Montpelier, and Fort Mims to a ferry that crossed the Alabama River at a place called Cut-Off. Another ferry at Blakeley also enabled travel in the area.

1806

Josiah Blakeley, described as "a bachelor of an enterprising disposition," arrives in Mobile by way of Santiago de Cuba.

1810

Joshua Kennedy's mill was built. Some fourteen sawmills were located in the northern half of Baldwin County and include Black's Mill, McDonald's Sawmill, Hills Sawmill, Watson's Sawmill, Robinson's Sawmill, Kennedy's Sawmill, Byrnes Mill and Hastie-Silver Mills.

1811

Travel gets easier when the early horse path procured from the Indians was widened into the wagon road that became "Three Chopped Way" or, as it was better known, "Three Notched Way." The name was derived from the fact that early highway markers were simply a set of notches etched into trees.

1813

Samuel Mims and several hundred others died in the Fort Mims massacre of August 30, 1813. Peter J. Hamilton, in *Colonial Mobile,* says of him that "it was the blood of grayheaded Sam Mims crying from the ground, and his spirit leading on, that opened the interior of Alabama to civilization."

As noted in Chapter 1, accounts vary, but historian Albert

Pickett claimed that some 550 people lost their lives in the Fort Mims massacre. Others say the death toll was around 250, excluding the Indians. Pickett writes a harrowing account of the battle:

> The bastion was broken down, the helpless inmates were butchered. Blood and brains bespattered the whole place. The children were seized by the legs and killed by beating their heads against the stockading. The women were scalped, and those who were pregnant were opened while they were alive and the embryo infants let out of the womb.

Two warriors held Samuel Mims while a third cut and peeled off the scalp. Then one of them mercifully crushed his skull with a warclub while another attached the scalp to a long pole, and holding it aloft, gleefully exhibited the long flowing white hair.

Portion of the reconstructed wall of Fort Mims, as seen from the nearby woods.

A Wedding in the Delta

Samuel Mims's history is associated with massacre, but a happier story links him with love and romance. It tells of a time before 1813 and reveals the courting practices of the day. Mims was giving a Christmas party at his home, and according to Kay Nuzum's account in *A History of Baldwin County,* young couples "paired off" at this time and lived together under a mutual promise to wed because magistrates did not make regular visits to the Delta. Marriages had to wait until a minister or magistrate traveling through the area was able to legalize the union. As time would have it, the story has been altered a bit, but it probably went something like this:

Daniel Johnson and Elizabeth Linder were, as the saying goes, a young couple "head-over-heels" in love. She was wealthy and came from a prominent family which may account for the invitation she and her lover received to Samuel Mims's Christmas soiree this particular December evening. Daniel was poor, and it is said that Elizabeth's parents would not condone a marriage they felt was beneath their daughter's station. Nevertheless, on this night when the weather had not yet turned chill and the party was getting in full swing, and all the invitees happily dancing, the women light on their toes and their gallant partners smiling and thinking of romance, Daniel took Elizabeth's hand and slipped out into the starlit night. Some friends joined them, whereupon they boarded canoes for a row on the river, traveled down Boatyard Lake into the Mobile River, canoed on to Fort Stoddard and then to Mobile. The journey took all night.

When the travelers arrived in Mobile at dawn, they found Captain Bartholomew Schaumburgh, commander of the fort, up early making eggnog. He was just preparing to pour in a plentiful dose of spirits when Daniel and Elizabeth turned up and asked that the captain join them in marriage.

"Umm," the commander said. "I don't have authority to perform ceremonies of this sort. I'm sorry."

"But sir," Daniel said. "If you'll remember, the United States government gives you authority as a general protector and regulator of affairs to do things that need to be done with sanction and adjustment. We would that you would join us in holy matrimony."

The commander smiled. It was, after all, the holiday season. The young suitor was handsome and persuasive, and so Schaumburgh stood before the couple and pronounced the vows.

"Will you, Daniel," he said, his voice deep, resonant and serious, "take Elizabeth as your lawful wedded wife? And will you, Elizabeth, take Daniel?" And so, on this early Christmas morning, the vows were exchanged and the couple pronounced man and wife.

"Go home now," the Captain said. "Behave yourselves, multiply, and replenish the Tensaw country."

Daniel and Elizabeth were radiant, even after their long night on the river. Captain Schaumburgh passed around the eggnog he'd just made; it was thoroughly laced with spirits. Everyone began a round of toasts. Daniel and Elizabeth toasted each other, toasted the captain, toasted their friends and only after appropriate celebrating did they make their way back to the waiting canoe. When the newlyweds arrived again at Mims's abode, those still present from the night before held another celebration and declared that, indeed, Daniel and Elizabeth were the best couple the Boatyard community had seen in a long, long time. It was deemed a truly merry Christmas, and the party sang out "Deck the halls with boughs of holly," and "Peace on earth, good will to men."

The Fort Mims massacre increased tensions between Indians in what is now the state of Alabama and white settlers who were increasingly moving into the region. Within seven months, the Creek Indian War came to a dramatic conclusion at the Battle of Horseshoe Bend in central Alabama, where forces commanded by Andrew Jackson effectively ended the Creek Nation.

1813

Josiah Blakeley bought the tract of land that was to become Blakeley. This was the realization of his dream, that of establishing a city that would be a marvelous seaport and place to live.

Lumbering was a major source of business income in the Mobile-Tensaw Delta. The first sawmill was built near Rain's Creek in the Stockton area.

1818

One of the first newspapers in Alabama, the semi-weekly *Blakeley Sun,* was published by Gabriel F. Mott.

1819

The first courthouse is built in Baldwin County. Prior to this, Judge Toulmin had sat up in a fork of a magnificent old oak and held court. The old tree became known as "the Jury Oak." Prisoners who were found guilty were taken nearby to another oak called "The Hanging Tree." The Jury Oak fell in 1992, and a memorial service was held to commemorate it as one of Alabama's first court sites. Landscape architect Mark Thomas estimated that the old tree was between four hundred and six

hundred years old, though it may have been dying for more than a century. "It was like a man who lived to be 150 years old," Thomas said. "No human intervention over the past hundred years could have saved the tree."

1819

A long extended moan splits the air and cuts into the silence of the night. It is a steamboat making its way on the Tensaw River, and boat building was an important industry of the day. According to Kay Nuzum, the steamboat era was one of the most romantic periods of Baldwin County and the Delta's history. Little boys dreamed of being steam boat captains.

The first Alabama steamboat was built at St. Stephens in 1818. *The Tensas,* with a capacity of two hundred bales of cotton, was built at Blakeley in 1819. *The Alpha,* built at Tensaw, was in operation around 1835. *The Wanderer, Narcissus,* and *Marengo,*

Modern Delta excursions are by kayak rather than steamboat.

July Sunday School excursion was a tumultuous event," complete with a calliope blaring out sacred songs as well as the hit songs of the day.

The aft quarters of the steamboats provided more prestigious staterooms, for they were situated some distance from the boilers. If the boat blew up, the passengers housed there were more apt to escape, not necessarily with their possessions, but with their lives. Deck passengers, however, slept anywhere they could find a spot among the bales of cotton and barrels of freight. But imagine for a moment that it is the late 1850s. You are standing on the deck of the steamboat *Narcissus* at night, the river is calm, the air cool, and the night stars overhead are simply thrilling. Music is heard, and you join in singing Stephen Folster's "Hard Times Come Again No More," singing the oddly prophetic lines:

> While we seek mirth and beauty and music light and gay
> There are frail forms fainting at the door:
> Though their voices are silent, their pleading looks will say—
> Oh! Hard Times, come again no more.

Little could it be known that the terrible siege of Blakeley would take place in only fifteen years. Little could it be known that, as the poet T. S. Eliot put it, time present and time past would be present in time future, and time future would be contained in time past. Hard times would come again all too soon. We experience a living history.

1820

A commission was appointed to purchase a suitable site and establish the Baldwin County seat of government at Blakeley, the cost of which was not to exceed $2,000.

A regular mail route began operation around this time along the Old Federal Road.

also built at Blakeley, were in service in 1836, 1844–1855, and 1856-1867 respectively. *STEAMBOAT K,* built at Stockton, operated around 1853-1859.

The more impressive steamboats boasted about providing "fashionable excursions." Nuzum reports that the "Fourth of

1821

The stagecoach business began to thrive in the Mobile-Tensaw Delta. Ward Taylor of Butler County and Patrick Byrne of Baldwin County formed a partnership with Major Johnson whose stagecoach brought the first mail from Georgia in 1821.

1832

Zechariah Godbold, who died in 1832, is the only Revolutionary War soldier known to be buried in Baldwin County soil. He was buried in Saluda Hill near Blakeley.

1834–1839

The town of Stockton in the Mobile-Tensaw Delta was founded in 1834 though it wasn't actually incorporated until 1839 when William Kitchen of Mobile joined with the town of Stockton with its quarter interest and paid $24,250 for a new stagecoach line. The mail on this line was delivered from Mobile to Pensacola, from Mobile to Montgomery, and from Mobile to Coffeeville, Demopolis, Livingston, Hayneville, and Braggston.

The fine stagecoaches were fitted with six-seat coaches. Some two hundred horses were stationed along the routes at intervals of sixteen to eighteen miles. This assured a ready supply of fresh horses to drive both people and the mail.

A four-horse team that made the 192-mile run to Montgomery was said to take approximately forty-three hours. Speaking of stagecoach serviceability, the Mobile *Daily Commercial Register* ran the following ad: "New coaches, good terms, and careful drivers will be found on the whole line. Eating houses are as good as the nature of the country."

One of Alabama's former Poet Laureates, Helen Blackshear writes convincingly of the days of the Creek Indians and stagecoaches in Alabama. "The Stagecoach Ride," one of the stories in

The Creek Captives and Other Alabama Stories, recounts the tale of Tuskoon Fixakoo's stagecoach ambush that took place on May 9, the account of which F. L. Cherry reported in his history of Opelika, 1886. Although Blackshear's story is not actually set in the Mobile-Tensaw Delta, it gives the tenor of the time when stagecoaches were traveling Alabama's trails, and though life

Stockton United Methodist Church sign celebrates area's rich history.

might be exciting, it was also dangerous and subject to Indian attack. Blackshear writes:

> The Injuns had sure enough been on a rampage. They'd burned the bridge on Big Uchee Creek over on the Old Federal Road, had killed Mr. McKizzie and his wife, and also had plundered Mr. Hartwell Green's wagon and killed his mules, though the family got away safe. Joseph Blake had been out with his boys rousin' the neighbors, and ten families was makin' up a caravan to head for Columbus come nightfall.

Lucille Griffiths recounts this raid in *Alabama: A Documentary History,* published by the University of Alabama Press in 1968. Another account of Alabama stagecoach days is included in M. W. Clinton's *Tuscaloosa, Alabama: Its Early Days,* published in 1958.

Reporting a local Indian attack, Kay Nuzum delineates a disturbance that occurred between the Creeks and the settlers that forced one stagecoach proprietor to live for more than a week on bread made from whiskey rather than from water or milk. Warring Indians, it is said, kept him from being able to go out to milk his cows or go the nearby spring for water. Perhaps it is little wonder, though, that our proprietor was able to endure. He had not only bread to eat, but bread spiced with fine spirits.

Nuzum says that because the area was sparsely settled, the life of a stagecoach proprietor could be frightening and lonely.

Charles Daniels, too, finds the stagecoach era one of fascination and importance. In "Reminiscences of Olden Times in Baldwin," he writes that:

> In 1841 the Government established a horseback express line which ran from Stockton by Montgomery Hill, Mt. Pleasant, Claiborne, Greenville, and Montgomery to Washington City.

Major Ward Taylor of Stockton and Wade Allen of Montgomery, were the contractors. This line was run daily for four years (I think). The riders were boys from 11 to 14 years old. Among them were James Hadley, Jesse Hadley, Simon Hadley and others whose names I can't recall now. The horses were changed every 10-12 miles and had to be run at a high rate of speed. One of the shortest runs was 7 miles from Stockton at what is now called Seven-Mile Springs. I have known these 7 miles to be run in less that 20 minutes to make connection with the mailboat at Stockton, and have known several horses to drop dead on the bluff at Stockton from exhaustion. It was said that 90 horses were required on the route between Stockton and Montgomery, and at the expiration of the four years, only two of the horses left were among those that were commenced with. The contractors were careful in selecting good stock. The usual rate of speed was 10 to 12 miles per hour. The mail was carried in a small rubber pouch buckled around the rider's waist, locked with a small brass lock. All letters were limited to one half ounce in weight, no newspapers, only little strips of important news cut out, rolled up in white paper sealed with wax at each end. Seventy-five cents was the amount charged for carrying parcels or letters on this route. In 1842 the writer of this, paid that price for letters received in New York from Alabama. This express line was subsequently run from Blakeley to Montgomery. The establishment of a telegraph line from New Orleans to Montgomery, broke up the horseback line.
>
> . . .

In spite of dangers and long days of bumpy travel, there were satisfactions to be had at the stagecoach stops. Blackshear's narrator in "The Stagecoach Ride" speaks of fine breakfasts that consisted of fried chicken, battercakes with molasses, and ham and eggs.

An early menu of the Stagecoach Cafe located on the Old

Federal Road gives a brief history of stage stops at Little River, Montgomery Hill, Stockton, and Patrick Byrnes Tavern near Blakeley. At Mrs. Bryant's tavern at Montgomery Hill, breakfasts could be had for fifty cents and supper for seventy-five cents. The latter might include chicken pie, ham, five vegetables, pudding and sauce, sweet pies, preserved fruits, deserts or strawberries, and plums, and wine or brandy.

The Stagecoach Cafe today still offers a savory repast. The menu boasts that their "special blend of spices" gives their broiled items "a unique and delicious flavor," while their "secret breading recipe" gives their fried seafood, especially catfish, "its original Stagecoach flavor."

1852

The area was struck by a hurricane.

1854

Mr. William Kitchen and his wife, Narcissia Watson, built a house in Stockton that featured an immense carriage house, an ancient barn, and a tiny post office.

1865

The Siege of Blakeley lasted from April 2 through 9, 1865. The Civil War ended with General Robert E. Lee's surrender to General Ulysses Grant on April 9 at Appomattox Courthouse in Virginia. The Battle of Blakely* took place only six hours after Lee's surrender.

Fort Blakely was an entrenchment built of nine connected earthen artillery redoubts that mounted forty-one artillery pieces. (*It is to be noted that Blakeley was the correct spelling of the town, whereas Fort Blakely was spelled without the final "e" during the Civil War.)

The U.S. commander during the siege was General E. R. S. Canby. The Confederate commander was Brigadier General John R. Liddell.

The Confederates held the fort for two weeks, until April 9, and sadly waited for reinforcements that never came.

Speaking of Blakeley in the foreword to an undated small publication, *The Siege of Blakeley and the Campaign of Mobile* by Roger B. Hansen and Norman A. Nicolson, Mary Y. Grice who retired as director for Historic Blakeley State Park in 1997, writes:

> The beauty of Blakeley exemplifies the quote: "To wake the soul by tender strokes of art, to raise the genius and to mend the heart." The terrain, the variety of trees, the beauty of the wild flowers, and the general environment of loveliness you will find no where else in our part of the country. When you walk upon its trails, you feel lost in time; when you smell its scents, you feel lifted out of yourself. Your heart expands, your soul is at peace. In short, you "Walk With God."
>
> Blakeley is a place where man has come and gone again . . . over and over . . . in at least four thousand years of history that we know about, and perhaps many more thousands that we don't yet know.
>
> The reason that man was drawn to Blakeley and was then gone again is the same reason that man now returns. Beauty. Environment. Accessibility. Today it lies between two major expressways, on the only connecting highway between the two.
>
> Blakeley's shoreline has a deep harbor that provides both fresh and salt water fish. The game is prolific. Voluminous amounts of water pour forth from its fresh-water spring. The soil is rich and gradually rises to a height of 180 feet above sea level. Blakeley is a natural paradise existing twelve miles from a major metropolitan center.
>
> "How blessed are we to be able to drive this short distance

from the stresses of life and be at peace." My determination has always been to give my fellow man the access to this enchanting landscape and historical property, so that he might have a place of beauty and tranquility to help him along the thorny paths of life.

1865

A yellow fever epidemic helped bring about the decline of Blakeley.

1868

The Baldwin County Board of Revenue Commission voted to move the county seat from Blakeley to Daphne where it remained until 1901.

1888

The population of Stockton registered four hundred people. The cypress swamps furnished plentiful material for building. Hauled by oxen and then later by mules, logs were taken to local sawmills and cut into lumber which was shipped by river and ocean to markets around the world.

1893

On October 2, a tropical storm caused water to back up in the rivers and caused flooding in the area. The storm caused damage to timber in the Delta.

1906

On September 27, a hurricane caused fourteen-foot tides in some areas along Mobile Bay. Water backed into the rivers that were said to have risen as much as ten feet about mean tide.

1916

July 5. A hurricane with 100 mile-an-hour winds caused 11.6 foot tides over the coastal area of Mobile and Baldwin County. Timber was severely damaged in the Delta.

1946

The National Defense Reserve Fleet which came to be known as "The Ghost Fleet," the "Mothball Fleet," and as "Baldwin's Barnacle Battle" was created by an act of Congress in 1946. It was located at Lower Hall's Landing on the Tensaw River, off Highway 255 and was one of eight such fleets in the United States. Following World War II, ships were brought into the Mobile River, but because of traffic and issues of available space, the ships were destined to be moved by means of a 1947 man-made canal that was dug between the Mobile and Tensaw rivers into the Tensaw River. Some 450 ships made up the fleet and were later thrust again into service in Korea and Viet Nam. Nuzum, in her report "Baldwin's Reserve Fleet," says that *The Douglas Victory* made five voyages to Viet Nam carrying cargo, but the ship was returned to the Delta in 1967. The purpose of storing the fleet was to use the ships' metal and the machinery. Nuzum describes the "Moth-balling":

> The preservation process consisted of scaling and thoroughly cleaning the ship's hull, deck, engines and electrical equipment, then coating all components with a preservative. Some were preserved through a "dehumidification" process. Underwater areas were protected from erosion by the "cathodic protection" system. This system works on the silverplating principle by applying an electric current through the water to the metallic hull of a ship. The electricity renders the hull steel inert, so that it will not combine with oxygen to form rust.

The Ghost Fleet significantly contributed to the economy of Baldwin County during the period after the war.

1966

Oil drilling occurred in the Delta. Robert A. (Bob) Lee established the Hubbard Landing Field that consisted of four producing wells, but there was a problem with pumping below 8,000 feet because the oil barrels also contained hot salt water. The oil could be separated from the water but an issue arose about the disposal of the salt water in an environmentally appropriate way. The field was shut down and the wells plugged.

1970

Calvin William McGhee, chief of the Creek Nation East of the Mississippi and great-great-great nephew of William Weatherford, was buried in the Poarch Indian community on June 13. A retired farmer, he was instrumental in procuring $3.9 million dollars from the Bureau of Indian Affairs for land in Alabama and Georgia that was taken from the Creeks after the War of 1812. McGee worked specifically for a better education for his people. In the early 1940s, children in the Poarch and Husford areas went to school in three-room church buildings in Poarch. Following McGhee's involvement, a new elementary school was built at Poarch.

1972

Red Eagle's grave site is deeded to Baldwin County.

1974

On June 14, the Causeway was officially dedicated. Dixie Graves, the wife of Governor Bibb Graves, opened a bottle of Satsuma juice on the Tensaw bridge.

1974

The Alabama Historical Commission nominates Blakeley for the National Register of Historic Places.

1985

Chesley Pruett, owner of an independent petroleum oil company, resumed oil drilling in the Delta at what was known as the Tensaw Lake Field.

1990

International Paper Company donated to the people of Alabama more than one thousand acres of the Civil War battlefield at Blakeley. This land was valued at $1.4 million dollars. The property, donated to the Blakeley Historical Foundation, is part of the 3,800-acre historical area located about twelve miles east of Mobile in Baldwin County.

1993

The Alabama Coastal Foundation (ACF) was formed to improve and protect the quality of Alabama's coastal resources by identifying and solving problems through education, cooperation, and participation.

1994

The South Alabama Birding Association, a non-profit corporation, was founded to promote bird conservation and the preservation of bird habitats, and to foster a greater understanding of birds through education, publication, and recreational birding activities.

1996

Blakeley was placed on the Civil War Trail by the National Civil War Trust.

1997

The Mobile Bay Watch (MBW) was formed to educate citizens and legislators in regard to standards that will enforce water quality laws and higher air and water emission standards that affect the health and quality of life of the area's citizenry.

1997

The Alabama Black Bear Alliance (ABBA) was formed to promote the restoration of the black bear into its former range in Alabama through education, research, and habitat. The group is affiliated with the Alabama Wildlife Federation and the Nature Conservancy of Alabama.

1998

Two-thirds of the Tensaw River received the state's highest protective designation by the unanimous vote of the Alabama Environmental Management Commission.

1998

The Forever Wild Land Trust paid more than $700,000 for 420 acres within the Blakeley State Park. This ensured that the area would be protected from development. The tract includes the Civil War earthen-works of both the Union and Confederate armies. It also includes Indian shell mounds, and an array of unusual plants and animals.

1999

Mobile Bay Watch's BayKeeper program was officially accepted into the national Water Keeper Alliance. The *Mobile Register* reports that Edward O. Wilson, while visiting the University of Alabama in May, commented that the fresh water available in Alabama is a treasure. Water may be more scarce in fifty years. "So, fellow Alabamians," he said, "consider yourself blessed, and protect and celebrate your aquatic treasure."

2000

SANE, the South Alabama Network for the Environment, is formed to establish a network of grassroots environmentalists in southern Alabama in order to further communication among local environmental organizations and thus facilitate working together to protect the local environment.

2003

State regulators "discovered new evidence of mercury-contaminated fish in a number of south Alabama streams." They specifically mentioned the Blackwater River in Baldwin County and the Middle River in the Mobile-Tensaw Delta. ↜

ISSUES OF PRESERVATION

A network of rivers, creeks, bays, lakes, wetlands, and bayous, the Mobile Tensaw-Delta area consists of some 20,323 acres of water. The beauty of the cypress swamps, the majesty of the marsh, and the extent of the bodies of water make the Delta a paradise for fishing, so the quality of the water is an environmental imperative.

Dr. Charles Rodning, a local surgeon and environmentalist, writes that "water is an apt and vivid metaphor for resolution of the dichotomy that exists between exploitation and preservation." He likens it to "oriental philosophic and artistic traditions" that reference the "mind like water" as it serves as a model for the human spirit. Rodning says in *Literary Mobile* that

> a mind as clear and reflective as water is a mind receptive and responsive to a source of energy and insight inclusive of, but also beyond, the senses—to an intuition, to an understanding, to a wisdom, to an enlightenment, to the Way. Such a mind recognizes an interdependence, interrelationship, and interweaving among all phenomena. . . . This implies an alignment with one's source and a maintenance of one's true essence, but it also acknowledges a need to be adaptive and responsive to one's circumstance and environment at each moment—acknowledging a need to be adaptive and responsive to the present in terms of space and time.

Now is relative as a concept of time, for "now" is constantly changing. Some of the concerns in the new millennium, however, are an approximate "now." The issues are largely environmental and address both maintenance and preservation. In *The Love of Nature and the End of the World: The Unspoken Dimen-sions of Environmental Concern,* Shierry Weber Nicholsen speaks of what she calls a "holding environment" which she defines as the "places where experiments meet adaptive challenges." She notes that "groups and meetings of all kinds, families, and the temporary intellectual community created by the internal dialogue between author and reader are instances of potential holding environments in which any participant may exercise a capacity for binocular vision at a particular point and in which new thought may arise as a result of reflection." Indeed, we need to examine what we can do as we determine "our relationship to the natural world and its deterioration."

In examining Nicholsen's words, the word "experiment" stands out. What does she mean by "experimenting" with our environment? Don't we need results instead of experiments? Nicholsen explains that "an adaptive challenge" is one in which we do not have ready answers, one where there is no certainty about outcomes. Any action, then, is an experiment. Even if we cannot accept actions taken in the past, they serve as a point of departure. They take us from a specific place and time to another view that would better serve present causes. Nicholsen provides an end and yet a new beginning to our valuations of the Mobile-Tensaw Delta. She writes that

> the new cannot emerge from imitation, but it can draw on the traditions—a form of holding environment—that provides gifts to those who follow them. But this means that each person, with the help of the holding environments he or she is lucky enough to have or to help create, generates his or her own thoughts and experiments.
>
> . . . Anyone in any position can exercise leadership, because each person in a particular role, identity, or niche in a group or society is well situated to try a specific kind of experiment on a given issue.

. . . We should foster the mental space that will allow for creative links to be made that can then become the basis for creative—and hence unpredictable and unprescribable—actions.

The Mobile-Tensaw Delta prompts environmental interest and accepts the challenges that bring new insight into issues of ecology. The Nature Conservancy works to protect the endangered species that make their home in the Delta and contributed $1 million toward the purchase of 47,000 acres by the Alabama Forever Wild Program. In addition, the Alabama Chapter of the Conservancy wrote a $940,000 National Coastal Wetlands grant specifically for land acquisition in the Delta. Ducks Unlimited generously provided matching funds of $250,000.

The Mobile Bay National Estuary Program (MBNEP) under the directorship of Captain David W. Yeager states that its mission is to maintain and promote wise stewardship of the water quality and living resources of the Mobile Bay and Delta through comprehensive conservation and management.

One project funded for May 2004 was the identification and distribution of harmful algae in relation to water quality parameters in Mobile Bay. A database enumerating the microalgal species that form harmful algae blooms is being assembled. The work at the Dauphin Island Sea Lab will provide both undergraduate and graduate course work.

Another funded project that directly relates to the Mobile-Tensaw Delta involves determining the effects of forest management edges on amphibian/reptile assemblages and toxicant loading. This project will identify species valuable in determining the effects of habitat fragmentation on the ecosystem health of the Mobile-Tensaw Delta.

Students of all ages are involved in environmental projects related to the well-being of the Delta. The Herpetofauna of Dauphin Island Project will inform visitors to and residents of the area about the different species of reptiles and amphibians that currently live on Dauphin Island and that also inhabit the region classified as the Mobile-Tensaw Delta. Wetland monitoring will be addressed. The project will reach out to the students of the Dauphin Island Elementary School and also to Elderhostel tour groups with an interest in environmental concerns.

Students at Gulf Shores High School will establish water tanks that will simulate Mobile Bay conditions. The project, "Restoring Grasses for Mobile Bay," will involve students' seeding and growing grassbeds associated with aquatic life.

Biology students and teachers from the Alabama School of Mathematics and Science will monitor and map water quality measurements, vegetation distributions, sedimentation, and land use within D'Olive Bay and/or the D'Olive Creek watershed as sedimentation. The project is entitled "Student Monitoring of Ecological Change in D'Olive Bay."

The Nature Conservancy has been working with a number of partners for over a decade to protect the area of the Mobile-Tensaw Delta. It works to benefit some sixty-seven rare, imperiled, threatened or endangered species that make their home in the lands and waters of the Delta. This includes the black bear, the American alligator and the Alabama red bellied turtle.

Finally, this book on the Mobile-Tensaw Delta results specifically from the Alabama Coastal Foundation's interest in educating the people of Alabama and the nation about the natural, historical, and cultural history of the Mobile-Tensaw Delta. The project had the sponsorship, too, of many individuals and ExxonMobil, the Crampton Trust, Mobile Bay National Estuary Program, Alabama State Port Authority, Alabama Power Foundation, Riviera Utilities, Taylor Engineering LLC, Dr. Lynn Yonge, Boan Contracting Company, Leatherbury Real Estate, Mobile Bay Audubon Society, the Nature Conservancy, and the U.S. Fish and Wildlife Service. ✍

Bibliography

Studying Nature:
Literature and the Environment

ECOCRITICISM is a word that asks how texts represent place and how they reveal what the environment means to those who are an integral part of it. A number of questions come immediately to mind and ask, in short, how we discuss and act upon important environmental and ecological issues. And in trying to understand the living environment, where do we start?

Let's begin with where we are in our daily life. What of nature is present in the surround? Psychologists say that replicating nature affords serenity, and hospitals today create spaces where family members and patients, if they are able, can walk and sit, indeed find peace among gardens that feature plants and ponds. At home we build birdhouses and arbors, construct waterfalls, and plant bushes, flowers, and trees. We try to get back to nature, putting potted plants on our window sills, flowers on the kitchen table, and hanging plants where we can. Just learning what will best grow where is a place to begin a study of nature.

The following are books that have played an important part in formulating the ideas that appear in *In The Realm Of Rivers.*

Abram, David. *The Spell Of The Sensuous: Perception and Language in a More-than-Human World, 1996.*

   An essential book for everyone's bookshelf. It marks the place where ecology meets philosophy, psychology, and history. To read this book is to be changed by it. If only one book could be read on the environment, perhaps this is it.

Anderson, Lorraine, Scott Slovic, and John P. O'Grady. *Literature and the Environment: A Reader on Nature and Culture.* New York: Longman, 1999.

Brings together an interesting selection of fiction, poetry, biography, and cultural commentary as it explains environmentalism.

Bartram, William. *Travels.* Philadelphia: James & Johnson, 1971.

Covers the author's travels into the Mobile-Tensaw Delta.

Berry, Wendell. *Standing by Words.* San Francisco: North Point Press, 1983.

A collection of essays in which the author addresses the way language enables human beings to restore balance, harmony, and coherence in their lives and in the land.

Blackshear, Helen F. *The Creek Captives And Other Alabama Stories.* Montgomery, Alabama: NewSouth Press, 2001

A collection of stories that provide insight into and valuable information about the Creek Indians of Alabama.

Coupe, Laurence, ed. *The Green Studies Reader: From Romanticism to Ecocriticism.* London and New York: Routledge, 2000.

A comprehensive survey of material that examines the connection between ecology, culture, and literature. Sue Walker uses this book as a text in her Literature and the Environment class.

Crawford, James M. *The Mobilian Trade Language.* Knoxville: University of Tennessee Press, 1978.

A ethnolohistorical study of the Indians of the Mississippi Valley.

Gaard, ed. *Ecofeminism: Women, Animals, Nature.* Philadelphia: Temple University Press.

Discusses the conflicts that exist between Green politics and ecofeminism.

Gilcrest, David W. *Greening the Lyre: Environmental Poetics and Ethics.* Reno: University of Nevada Press, 2002.

A book that connects poetic inspiration with environmentalism.

Glotfelty and Harold Fromm, Eds. *Ecocriticism Reader.* Athens: University of Georgia Press, 1996.

A fine collection of essays that addresses the field of literary ecology. It provides a good introduction to the field and sketches its development over the past quarter-century.

Goodrow, Sister Esther Marie. *Mobile During The Civil War.* Mobile: Historic Mobile Preservation Society, 1950.

A book that addresses the contributions to the Confederacy, the role of the Catholics, and the taking of Mobile, and Mobile under Northern occupation.

Hastie, Lynn. *William Weatherford: His Country and His People.* A thorough and compelling biography of William Weatherford.

Newcomb Comings and Martha M. Albers. *A Brief History of Baldwin County.* Fairhope, Alabama: Baldwin Country Historical Society, 1928.

An interesting survey of the history of Baldwin County, much of which relates to the history of the Mobile-Tensaw Delta.

Nicholsen, Shierry Weber. *The Love of Nature and the End of the World.* Cambridge: The MIT Press, 2002.

This book is a gathering of meditations and collages that addresses the challenges of living fully and well in a world of potential environmental destruction. Nicholsen references such well known philosophers, ecologists, and psychoanalysts as Wilfred Bion, Donald Meltzer, and D.W. Winnicott.

Nuzum, Kay. *A History of Baldwin County.* Fairhope, Alabama: Eastern Shore Publishing Company, 1971.

An invaluable source of information about the history of Baldwin Country and the history and culture of the Mobile-Tensaw Delta.

Oelschlaeger, Max. *The Idea of Wilderness: From Prehistory to the Age of Ecology.* New Haven: Yale University Press, 1991.
Shows how the concept of wild nature has changed over the millennia.

Oliver, Mary.
Any book of poetry or essay collection. Anyone interested in nature and how to live with and in nature must read Mary Oliver.

Orr, David W. *Earth in Mind: On Education, Environment, and the Human Prospect.* Washington, DC: Island Press 1994.
An important book that addresses economic, ecological, and educational concerns as they relate to environmental issues.

Pickett, Albert James. *History of Alabama.* Originally printed by Roberts & Son of Birmingham in 1896.
A book that is fascinating to read and an important source of Alabama history.

Plotkin, Mark. *Tales Of A Shaman's Apprentice: An Ethnobotanist Searches for New Medicines in the Amazon Rain Forest.* New York, Viking, 1993.
Presents an account of the connections between botany, anthropology, tropical medicine, shamanism and environmental conservation.

Rolston, Holmes, III. *Environmental Ethics: Duties to and Values in The Natural World.* Philadelphia: Temple University Press, 1988.
An solid introduction to environmental ethics.

Snyder, Gary. *The Practice of the Wild.* San Francisco: North Point Press, 1990.
A series of essays exploring the meaning of freedom, wildness, goodness, and grace as they define nature and the environment.

Wilson, E. O. *On Human Nature.* Cambridge: Harvard University Press, 1978.
A biologist's explanation of the relationship between science, man and society.

_____ *The Diversity of Life.* Cambridge: Harvard Press, 1992.
A call for stewardship and action that will enhance rather than diminish the quality of life on earth.

_____ *Naturalist.* New York: Warner Books, 1994.
Covers the author's young life in Alabama and particularly in Mobile.

_____ *In Search Of Nature.* Washington, D.C.: Island Press, 1996.
A study of animals in their natural setting and their relationship with their environments.

_____ *Consilience: The Unity of Knowledge,* 1999.
An important book that addresses the ways in which sociology, economics, the arts and religion are conjoined in a pursuit of unified knowledge.

_____ *The Future of Life.* New York: Alfred A. Knopf, 2002.
Addresses the ecological plight in relation to the earth's future.

Wolfe, Cary. *Animal Rites: American Culture, the Discourse of Species and Posthumanist Theory.* Chicago: University of Chicago Press, 2003.
Examines current notions of humanism and ethics.

Zimmerman, Michael E. *Contesting Earth's Future: Radical Ecology and Postmodernity.* Berleley: University of California Press, 1994.
Links environmental philosophy and Continental thought. ✍

By Dennis Holt

Photographer's Notebook

To illustrate and display this natural world in its undisturbed beauty, a nature photographer's first responsibility is to protect and assure the safety and well-being of the photographic subjects. In an ideal world it would be great if every picture opportunity had perfect light. But when working in wilderness areas, one of the biggest challenges is capturing your subject in good light. Occasionally a tripod or fill flash can be used. But working in and out of this hot, wet and humid swamp area and when many of your subjects are moving, flying or running, the use of a flash or tripod is almost impossible to maneuver.

When capturing the images in the Mobile Tensaw Delta, most of the photos are captured without the use of artificial or studio lights. The ideal illumination or best light for outdoor and nature photography is what many photographer's refer to as "the Golden Light," which usually occurs twice daily around sunrise and sunset. This light may a few minutes or a couple of hours, depending on the weather conditions.

Since this book consists of photos taken over the period of almost twenty years, a wide variety of cameras and film were used. All of the photos were taken with 35mm Nikon F series film cameras or the Nikon digital cameras. The film used was Kodak's Kodachrome 25 and 64 and Fujichrome Velvia 50 and Provia

100F. Shooting the photographs in this book was a labor of love for me. For those readers who are interested in some of the specifics of how the photos were made, here is some background on some of the photographs in this book:

Pages 2-3: This photo of the lower delta and the city of Mobile on the horizon with car lights on the Causeway was actually an afterthought. The day had become cloudy and I assumed my photography for the day was complete. Returning from the upper delta, I called my wife and some friends to ask if we could meet for dinner overlooking the lower Delta. After watching the clouds cover the sky and the light of the sunset, we finished our meal and were headed to our car. It was about thirty minutes after the scheduled sunset and suddenly the sky began to

turn red. I grabbed my camera and headed down the bank from the restaurant parking lot and snapped the photo. I had Fuji Velvia 50 film in the camera but did not record the exposure. Two lessons learned: First always have your camera available, and secondly some of the best sunset photos are taken thirty minutes to even an hour after sunset.

Page 4: I almost missed seeing this Tri-colored Heron. Luckily the movement of its white body against the black background caught my attention. This bird was fishing for minnows. His head was perfectly still and motionless for a good view of the fish below the water without reflection. But the rest of his body would move from right to left to make the fish move into position for

the catch. It was fascinating to watch this expert fisherman in its daily food gathering perfection. As always with all wildlife I focused on his eyes. The photo was hand-held without the use of a tripod, at 1/60 second at f5.6. Notice the eye is in perfect focus, although you may pick up a little movement in the body.

Page 6: A "gator hole" is a swamp term for a territorial body of water that an alligator uses as its home base. I found one gator hole that I often check whenever possible as there is a huge 10 to 12 foot alligator that lives in the area and at times can be seen sunning on the bank. If I stalk or walk slowly to his pond and

with luck and the right light, occasionally I have been able to capture him on film. This particular shot was snapped quickly as he sensed my presence and was easing back into the safety of his residence. This shot was hand-

held with good light at 1/125 second at f5.6. The film was Kodachrome 64.

Page 12: The hiding tree is a wonderful old tree located at Blakeley State Park and was said to be a hiding area and life saver for many Confederate soldiers during the Battle of Blakeley. I photographed this tree using a 24mm lens on a Nikon F4S camera mounted on a tripod, using Fujichrome Velvia 50 film.

Page 15: This old-growth Bald Cypress swamp is on Briar Lake north of Stockton. Photographed from a boat using a 35mm lens on a Nikon F4S camera using Fujichrome Velvia 50 film. Exposure was 1/125 at f11.

Page 16: The large photo of the lower delta marsh wetland was photographed from a bluff using Fujichrome Velvia 50 film with an exposure of a 1/60 second at f16. The smaller photo is cattle egrets wearing their yellow breeding plumage. The birds usually nest in colonies for protection. Most rookeries in the delta are in remote areas. I travel to these nesting areas with an expert or ornithologist studying the birdlife and their habitat. Remem-

ber to keep your distance and do not disturb the nesting process. I photographed these birds with a Nikon 500mm lens on a Nikon F4S camera from a tripod, using Fujichrome Velvia 50 film.

Page 17: The butterfly was caught with a Nikon 500mm lens on a tripod-mounted Nikon F4S and Fuji Velvia 50 film. I was set up to photograph the button bush when the butterfly landed on the flower. In nature photography, luck plays an important role.

Page 19: The photo of the canoe platform under the light of the full moon started with a phone call from friend and kayak enthusiast Bob Andrews. A small group from the Mobile Kayak and Canoe Club were planning a trip on the Bartram canoe trail and invited me. Now to many, canoeing at night in a swamp with snakes and alligators doesn't sound like any picnic. But to me it was an invitation for some interesting photography. Our trip began at Rice Landing about dusk. We headed toward Jug Lake where a new overnight canoe platform had just been completed. It was only about four and a half miles, or a 90-minute paddle. The eight of us reached the floating platform and enjoyed an informal potluck dinner—serenaded by a group of barred owls. The bright full moon came into view through the thick cypress trees and would soon be overhead. Bob and I grabbed my photo

equipment and paddled out looking for a good spot for a timed exposure of the platform. The foundation for the tripod needed to be solid ground, to keep the picture sharp and in focus. Unfortunately, Bob and I could not find any solid ground in this water world. So we had to improvise. We paddled up next to a huge cypress

tree and while I stood the tripod in the bottom of the unstable canoe, Bob tied us to the cypress tree. We knew that any movement while the shutter was open would ruin the photo. We had to keep the camera steady during the exposure! The moon is bright and needs no long exposure. But to capture the people on the platform with only the dim light of the lanterns required a time exposure. That created another film problem. If anyone moved during the extended exposure, they would be blurred. We were too far away to use just a flash and it would ruin the entire effect. So here is what we did. When the moon was in the right location and I gave the signal, Bob hugged the tree to hold us steady and we both froze and held our breath. I then exposed the film for three seconds and lagged the shutter after a quick fill flash. The flash was just quick enough to freeze the people for 1/60th of a second while the shutter stayed open for the remainder of the three seconds. This technique captured the moon, the lanterns, the platform, and the reflection of everything in the water. Bob had to pick the bugs and moss off himself from hugging the tree, but we got our picture. And all was in focus.

Page 171: I have to claim artistic license for this picture, as it was taken outside the bounds of what is considered the Tensaw Delta. The American alligator builds her nest in remote locations and with native grass and materials that help camouflage the nest from predators. For these reasons, the nest are rarely seen by people. This nest was accidentally discovered by a friend who was canoeing during an Audubon bird survey. To photograph the nest, I built a blind on the  deck of a flat-bottomed john boat. I moved this boat gradually into position over several days, then entered the blind each day over a two-week period. Many alligator nests are preyed upon and the eggs eaten by raccoons and bears. During one of my long days in the photo blind, I caught a glimpse of something moving to my left. As I quickly looked over my shoulder at the movement I accidentally dropped a drink cup on the floor of the aluminum boat, making a loud noise. As I moved my camera around I realized it was a black bear. The bear heard my movement and scampered away. Because of my presence, this alligator nest was probably spared from being destroyed. Oh yes, I did capture a photo of the bear, but it was just a dark blur.

Page 71: Nearly all black bears I've encountered in the Tensaw Delta area have not been deep in the middle of the swamp, but rather

near human-populated areas. Numerous people who think their trash cans are turned over nightly by dogs or raccoons would be surprised to discover that the culprit is a black bear. I've learned that the best way to photograph the Delta bear is from a photo blind, set up near trash cans at the edge of the swamp, near or on private property. The major problem in photographing black bears is that they are nocturnal and it's hard to capture them on film during good light. For this photo, my blind was set up near where I had seen tracks. Early one morning, two young black bears came into sight, and both climbed a tree near an opening

above the thick Titi bushes. Their dark fur, with the early morning light as the background, made them look like silhouettes. But in a situation like this, you must shoot and just hope for the best. I was shooting Velvia Provia 100 film in my Nikon 4FS with a Nikkor 300mm lens. I shot wide open with the lens at f/4 at 1/60th of a second. The resulting photos were darker than I wanted, but thanks to modern digital technology, I was able to digitize the film frame and adjust the photo in Adobe Photoshop. I usually refer to such digital asjustments as "Creative Interpretation."

Page 57: The ribbon snake is beautiful but rare. The first one I ever encountered was on Mound Island deep in the Delta. It made a quick dash across the foot path and then paused a moment before rushing away. It was just enough time

for me to catch a quick glance with my eyes, but not enough time to capture a good photograph. It's amazing but every trip I ever made to Mound Island afterwards, I have always managed to see the ribbon snake. I have many blurred streaks of color to prove it. But I needed a good identification photo for the delta book. So I called on some help from a reptile expert. Dr. David Nelson, a professor of Biology at the University of South Alabama, helped me with a captured ribbon snake under controlled conditions for this I.D. photo. Although Dr. Nelson is featured in this book, we first met as we both were working on Mound Island on a hot, humid and mosquito-infested July day. I was photographing the Indian Mounds and he was working with USA biology students. Meeting Dr Nelson in the field was good luck; he helped me capture many needed photos. A natural history photographer must devote a huge amount of time, have patience, luck in the

Index of Interviewees and Poem and Story Titles

INDEX

Opposite: *spider lily.*
Overleaf: *moss-covered tree at sunset.*